Quality Management for IT Services

IT Infrastructure Library

Brian Johnson
Martin Andrew
David Steel

London: HMSO

© Crown Copyright 1994

Applications for reproduction
should be made to HMSO

Second impression 1995

ISBN   0 11 330555 9
ISSN   0956-2591

This is one of the books in the IT Infrastructure
Library series.

For futher information on other CCTA
products, contact:

CCTA Library
Rosebery Court
St Andrews Business Park
Norwich, NR7 0HS

This document has been produced using
procedures conforming to
BS 5750 Part 1: 1987; ISO 9001: 1987.

Table of contents

1.	**Management summary**	**1**
1.1	About this module	1
1.2	Benefits	2
1.3	ISO 9001	2
2.	**Introduction**	**3**
2.1	Quality management	3
2.2	Purpose	3
2.3	Target readership	3
2.4	Scope	3
2.5	Related guidance	4
2.6	Standards	5
3.	**Planning for IT Services quality management**	**9**
3.1	Procedures	9
3.1.1	Overview	9
3.1.2	Appoint an Executive Sponsor	10
3.1.3	Conduct a feasibility study	11
3.1.4	Decide the scope of the Quality Initiative	16
3.1.5	Establish the Quality Steering Committee	17
3.1.6	Appoint a Quality Manager	17
3.1.7	Define IT Services quality philosophy, policies and goals	18
3.1.8	Plan the Quality Initiative	20
3.2	Dependencies	24
3.3	People	24
3.3.1	Organization	24
3.3.2	Staffing	27
3.3.3	Training	32
3.4	Timing	33
3.4.1	Feasibility study	33
3.4.2	Quality Steering Committee	33
3.4.3	Quality Manager	33

3.4.4	Quality goals	33
3.4.5	Quality office	33

4. Implementation — 35

4.1 Procedures — 35

4.1.1	Stage 1 - Initiation	35
4.1.2	Stage 2 - Analysis of QMS requirements	37
4.1.3	Stage 3 - Development of the QMS	38
4.1.4	Stage 4 - Installation of the QMS	46

4.2 Dependencies — 48

4.3 People — 48

4.4 Timing — 48

4.4.1	Timescales	49

5. Post-implementation and audit — 51

5.1 Procedures — 51

5.1.1	Project evaluation review	51
5.1.2	Post-implementation review	52
5.1.3	Management review and internal quality audit	52
5.1.4	Customer contract review	56
5.1.5	Service design	57
5.1.6	Service quality monitoring and control	57
5.1.7	Configuration management and change management	59
5.1.8	Quality improvement	59
5.1.9	Training	60
5.1.10	ISO 9001 certification	60

5.2 Dependencies — 61

5.3 People — 61

5.4 Timing — 62

6. Benefits, costs and possible problems — 65

6.1 Benefits — 65

6.1.1	Benefits to IT Services	65
6.1.2	Benefits to customers	66

6.2 Costs — 67

6.2.1	Planning, development and installation costs	67
6.2.2	Ongoing running costs	68
6.2.3	The costs of quality improvement	68

6.3	Possible problems	68
7.	**Tools**	**71**
8.	**Bibliography**	**73**

Annexes

A.	**Glossary of terms**	**A1**
B.	**Relevant International and British Standards**	**B1**
B.1	Relationships between British and International quality standards	B4
C.	**Quality and IT service concepts**	**C1**
C.1	Quality concepts	C1
C.2	IT service concepts	C6
D.	**Relevant quality initiatives**	**D1**
D.1	The Citizen's Charter	D1
D.2	Competing for quality	D1
D.3	The TickIT Project	D2
D.4	Vision 2000	D3
E.	**Applying ISO 9001 to IT Services**	**E1**
E.1	Management responsibility	E1
E.2	Quality system	E6
E.3	Contract review	E7
E.4	Design control	E9
E.5	Document control	E14
E.6	Purchasing	E16
E.7	Purchaser supplied product	E20

IT Infrastructure Library
Quality Management for IT Services

E.8	Product identification and traceability	E20
E.9	Process control	E21
E.10	Inspection and testing	E21
E.11	Inspection, measuring and test equipment	E23
E.12	Inspection and test status	E24
E.13	Control of nonconforming product	E24
E.14	Corrective action	E25
E.15	Handling, storage, packaging and delivery	E25
E.16	Quality records	E25
E.17	Internal quality audits	E26
E.18	Training	E26
E.19	Servicing	E27
E.20	Statistical techniques	E27
F.	**How the ITIL functions and modules relate to ISO 9000**	**F1**
F.1	Availability Management	F2
F.2	Capacity Management	F5
F.3	Change Management	F8
F.4	Computer Installation and Acceptance	F10
F.5	Computer Operations Management	F12
F.6	Configuration Management	F13
F.7	Contingency Planning	F16
F.8	Cost Management	F17
F.9	Customer Liaison	F18
F.10	Help Desk	F19
F.11	IT Services Organization	F21
F.12	Management of Local Processors and Terminals	F22
F.13	Managing Facilities Management	F23

F.14	Network Services Management	F24
F.15	Planning and Control	F25
F.16	Problem Management	F26
F.17	Service Level Management	F28
F.18	Software Control and Distribution Management	F31
F.19	Software Lifecycle Support	F31
F.20	Supplier Management	F32
F.21	Testing Software for Operational Use	F33
F.22	Third Party and Single Source Maintenance Management	F35
G.	**ISO 9000 certification**	**G1**
G.1	Accreditation	G1
G.2	Certification	G1
G.3	Assessment	G2
H.	**Types of quality audit**	**H1**
H.1	First party audits	H1
H.2	Second party audits	H2
H.3	Third party audits	H2
I.	**Interdependence of ITIL functions/modules**	**I1**
I.1	Availability management	I1
I.2	Capacity management	I3
I.3	Change management	I5
I.4	Computer installation and acceptance	I5
I.5	Computer operations management	I5
I.6	Configuration management	I7
I.7	Contingency planning	I7

I.8	Cost management	I8
I.9	Customer liaison	I8
I.10	Help desk	I9
I.11	IT Services organization	I9
I.12	Management of local processors and terminals	I10
I.13	Managing facilities management	I10
I.14	Managing supplier relationships	I10
I.15	Network services management	I10
I.16	Operational testing management	I11
I.17	Planning and control	I11
I.18	Problem management	I11
I.19	Service level management	I12
I.20	Software control and distribution	I12
I.21	Software lifecycle support	I12
I.22	Testing an IT service for operational use	I13
I.23	Third party and single source maintenance	I13
J.	**IT service quality characteristics**	**J1**

Foreword

Welcome to the IT Infrastructure Library module on **Quality Management for IT Services.**

In their respective areas the IT Infrastructure Library publications complement and provide more detail than the IS Guides.

The ethos behind the development of the IT Infrastructure Library is the recognition that organizations are becoming increasingly dependent on IT in order to satisfy their corporate aims and meet their business needs. This growing dependency leads to growing requirement for quality IT services. In this context quality means 'matched to business needs and user requirements as these evolve'.

This module is one of a series of codes of practice intended to facilitate the quality management of IT services and of the IT Infrastructure. (By IT Infrastructure, we mean organizations' computers and networks - hardware, software and computer related communications, upon which application systems and IT services are built and run). The codes of practice will assist organizations to provide quality IT services in the face of skill shortages, system complexity, rapid change, growing user expectations, current and future user requirements.

Underpinning the IT Infrastructure is the Environmental Infrastructure upon which it is built. Environmental topics are covered in separate sets of guides within the IT Infrastructure Library.

IT service management is a complex subject which for presentational and practical reasons has been broken down within the IT Infrastructure Library into a series of modules. A complete list of current and planned modules is available from the CCTA IT Infrastructure Management Services at the address given at the back of this module.

Consistency versus new challenges

The IT Infrastructure Library has been produced over a period of five years during which there have been significant changes in the business environment of Central Government. Major initiatives such as Next Steps, Citizen's Charter and Competing for Quality are affecting the organization of Departments and the way in which they conduct their business. These changes are having a significant effect on the IT Directorate.

IT Infrastructure Library
Quality Management for IT Services

The production of later volumes of the IT Infrastructure Library has therefore presented the dual challenges of maintaining consistency with earlier publications while ensuring relevance to today's Government departments. Both the changes in the Government department business environment and latest thinking in IT service management need to be taken into account. For example, the impact of market testing is addressed in the later books, even though the Competing for Quality White Paper had not been issued when the early books were published.

Some of the challenges which IT service suppliers face are:

* meeting requirements specified by the customer
* improved timeliness of response to customer needs
* cutting costs to provide economic, competitively priced services
* a clear separation of supply (provider of services) and demand (customer of services) with defined interfaces, regardless of whether or not the supply is in-house
* devolution of authority and budgets enabling the customer to decide which IT service suppliers to use.

Many of these issues have been identified and addressed in earlier volumes of the IT Infrastructure Library. However, changes in the business environment have provided new focus and emphasis which is particularly evident in this and other recent volumes. Further information is available in CCTA's Market Testing IS/IT publications.

Common themes and relationships in the IT Infrastructure Library

Three closely related modules in the Managers' Set of the IT Infrastructure Library provide additional information about common themes which run through all other modules in the Library: IT Services Organization, Planning and Control for IT Services and Quality Management for IT Services. These books give three different viewpoints or ways of looking at the IT Services organization:

* **IT Services Organization** concentrates on organizational structure, describes roles, skills and experience required by people, and provides a framework for reviewing the organizational structure to meet changing circumstances

Foreword

* **Planning and Control for IT Services** covers information flows and the development of an appropriate planning and control system to meet the requirements of the organization; people are one of the resources to be considered and the organizational structure will influence information flows, but the module has a wider focus covering all aspects of planning and control

* **Quality Management for IT Services** is concerned with putting in place an ISO9001 conformant quality management system; it encompasses organizational and planning and control aspects, since they are covered by the ISO9001 standard, but refers to the above two modules rather than repeating information.

In general, the three modules answer the following questions:

* who and where?

  - IT Services Organization

* what and when?

  - Planning and Control for IT Services

* what, why and how?

  - Quality Management for IT Services.

The three modules address distinct but closely related aspects of IT service management. Organizations using the IT Infrastructure Library may choose to use the three modules as part of a coordinated project. In particular, changes to organizational structure and the development of planning and control processes will often need to be considered in parallel. In addition, many organizations seek to develop procedures in line with the ISO9001 quality management standard which covers organizational issues and the use of plans and controls, but has a wider scope and refers to policies and standards, detailed procedures, agreements with the customer and document control.

The close links between the subject matters of these three modules, and indeed with others in the Library, means that there is a degree of overlap. Nevertheless these three modules present different but valid viewpoints of managing IT Services.

IT Infrastructure Library
Quality Management for IT Services

The structure of the module is, in essence:

* a **Management summary** aimed at senior managers (Directors of IT and above, typically down to Civil Service Grade 5), senior IT staff and, in some cases, users or office managers (typically Civil Service Grades 5 to 7)

* the main body of the text, aimed at IT middle management (typically grades 7 to HEO)

* technical detail in Annexes.

The module gives the main **guidance** in sections 3 to 5; explains the **benefits, costs and possible problems** in section 6, which may be of interest to senior staff; and provides information on **tools** (requirements and examples of real-life availability) in section 7.

CCTA is working with the IT industry to foster the development of software tools to underpin the guidance contained within the codes of practice (ie to make adherence to the module more practicable), and ultimately to automate functions.

If you have any comments on this or other modules, do please let us know. A **Comments sheet** is provided with every module. Alternatively you may wish to contact us directly using the reference point given in **Further information**.

Thank you. We hope you find this module useful.

Acknowledgement

The assistance of the following contributors is gratefully acknowledged:

ITMS Ltd.

Christine Ashby (CCTA)

Section 1
Management summary

1. Management summary

Information systems are increasingly important to the performance of organizations and large sums of money are spent on providing them. Most organizations spend more on IT service delivery and maintenance over the lifecycle of a service than on its development. It is imperative that users of those IT services obtain value for money. And of course IT services must be flexible, being matched to business needs and customer requirements as they evolve. IT services must also be provided economically, making optimum use of IT skills. There is increasing pressure on many organizations - particularly in government - to reduce costs while maintaining or improving IT services. A quality management system can assist with this process.

1.1 About this module

This module provides guidance to organizations on how to plan and implement a quality management system for IT Services that conforms to the requirements of the international quality standard ISO 9001, *Quality systems - Model for quality assurance in design/development, production, installation and servicing*, and the best practices for IT service management encapsulated in the IT Infrastructure Library. It is based on the CCTA Quality Management Library, which provides more detail on the quality issues discussed.

An initiative to improve IT Services quality by introducing a quality management system requires management commitment to succeed. The first step in planning quality improvement is the appointment of a senior manager as the *Executive Sponsor* who is the embodiment of that commitment. The Executive Sponsor will commission or conduct a feasibility study to establish the likely costs and benefits of the initiative, and to plan how to proceed.

It is recommended that the initiative should be planned and controlled using formal project management methods including a management board (known as the Quality Steering Committee) and a Project Manager.

A quality philosophy, policies and goals for IT Services are then defined and the implementation planned. The implementation activities include the analysis of quality management system (QMS) requirements, the development of the QMS and its introduction.

There are two major products of the initiative: the documented policies, procedures and standards which comprise the QMS; and the change in IT Services culture which will ensure that the new system is effective.

Once the QMS is in place, ISO 9001 certification may be sought to demonstrate that an effective QMS has been implemented and is being maintained. Whether or not the QMS is certified, on-going quality improvement should be an objective.

1.2 Benefits

The principal benefits of quality management for IT Services are a reduction in unnecessary costs - both for the service provider, and for the user - and increased user satisfaction.

The costs to an organization of poor quality IT services are high. Service failures lead to delays and costly rework by users; and IT services which do not support the business or users as effectively and efficiently as they could, impair the quality of the products or services of the organization and increase their cost.

An effective quality management system also gives users the confidence that IT Services will be able to fulfil its commitments and consistently provide services that satisfy their requirements.

Organizations which introduce quality management systems find that the cost of developing and introducing them is more than covered by the benefits obtained.

1.3 ISO 9001

ISO 9001 is one of a set of internationally agreed quality management and quality assurance standards which specifies the requirements for a quality management system for a supplier with the capability to design and deliver a service. ISO 9001 is identical to the British quality standard BS5750 part 1 and to the European standard EN 29001.

2. Introduction

2.1 Quality management

Quality management for IT Services is a systematic way of ensuring that all the activities necessary to design, develop and implement IT services which satisfy the requirements of the organization and of users take place as planned and that the activities are carried out cost effectively.

The way that an organization plans to manage its operations so that it delivers quality services, is specified by its quality management system. The quality management system defines the organizational structure, responsibilities, policies, procedures, processes, standards and resources required to deliver quality IT services. However, a quality management system will only function as intended if management and staff are committed to achieving its objectives.

2.2 Purpose

The purpose of this module is to provide guidance to help IT Services to plan, implement, maintain and improve a quality management system (QMS) for IT services which conforms to the requirements of the international standard for such systems: ISO 9001, *Quality systems - Model for quality assurance in design/development, production, installation and servicing*, and related guidance (see sections 2.4 and 2.5).

2.3 Target readership

The module is aimed at IS Directors, Quality Managers, IT Service Managers, Application Development and Application Maintenance Managers and all staff engaged in the provision or support of IT services.

The module will also be of interest to Facilities Management suppliers, auditors (internal or external) of quality management systems for IT services, and users of IT services who wish to help to ensure that they receive the quality of service that they deserve.

2.4 Scope

This module provides a framework for the development of a coherent and consistent QMS based upon the functions outlined in other IT Infrastructure Library modules. It therefore contains numerous cross-references to other IT Infrastructure Library modules and the CCTA Quality Management Library (in future referred to as the QML) in order to minimise duplication.

The IT Infrastructure Library
Quality Management for IT Services

The guidance applies to any organization supplying IT services. It can be applied to IT Services departments providing services to customers within the same organization or to IT services providers selling their services in the marketplace.

Some guidance is given (in section 4.4) on the sequence in which the parts of the quality management system relating to individual IT service management functions may best be implemented, but since each organization will have its own starting point, business requirements and constraints, each QMS implementation should be individually planned.

It is assumed that an ISO 9001 conformant quality management system will be implemented throughout the organization and reference is made to activities and people outside the scope of IT service management which could affect the quality of IT service provision. However developing a QMS for parts of the organization outside IT service management is excluded from this module. Specifically excluded from the scope of this module are QMS requirements for:

* application software development up to the point at which software is handed over to IT Services' control

* application code maintenance up to the point of hand over to IT Services' control following changes

* developing and giving training to the users of new IT services.

If desired, conformance to ISO 9001 and the effectiveness of the QMS may be recognised formally by certification by an accredited certification body (see Annex G for details of certification and accreditation).

The introduction of a QMS should be regarded as the beginning of the quality improvement process rather than the end. Ideally, the introduction of an ISO 9001 conformant QMS will be only one element of an overall Total Quality Management (TQM) programme.

2.5 Related guidance

This module is one of a series that constitutes the CCTA **IT Infrastructure Library**. Although the module can be read in isolation, it is recommended that it is used in conjunction with other modules, particularly those from the managers, service support, service delivery, software support, networks and computer operations sets. (A list of the relevant modules is given in Annex F, and the interrelationships between the various modules are discussed in Annex I.)

Each IT Infrastructure Library module gives guidance on best practice for a particular aspect of the provision of well managed IT services. If this guidance is implemented in its entirety, then the IT Services organization will have put the majority of the requirements of a QMS in place. This **Quality Management for IT Services** module refers to the other IT Infrastructure Library modules emphasising the importance of each volume to the overall QMS. (Bold type is used throughout this module when other IT Infrastructure Library modules are referred to.)

CCTA Quality Management Library

The module is based on advice given in the CCTA Quality Management Library (QML); in particular, the *Quality Management System Implementation* and *Quality Management System Audit* volumes of the library.

The QMS Implementation volume provides a step-by-step approach to the introduction of a QMS to all or any part or function of an IS organization. This IT Infrastructure Library module develops this general approach into a statement of what must be done to plan, implement and maintain a QMS for IT Services.

The QMS Audit volume provides guidance on the implementation of the audit function for IS in general. This module interprets the guidance for auditing IT service provision in particular.

Other volumes in the Quality Management Library provide complementary information about quality management systems in general, and about quality training and techniques.

2.6 Standards

ISO 9000/BS 5750/EN 29000 - Quality Management and Quality Assurance Standards

The IT Infrastructure Library modules are being designed to assist adherents (for example organizations' IT Directorates) to obtain third-party quality certification to ISO 9001. Such third-parties should be accredited by the NACCB, the National Accreditation Council for Certification Bodies.

ISO 9001 is part of the ISO 9000 series of standards which is identical to the BS (British Standard) 5750 and EN (European Norm) 29000 series of standards. The ISO 9000 reference numbers are used throughout this module (except where no ISO equivalent to a British standard exists, eg BS 5750 part 4). References to relevant sections of the standards are given in the form *ISO 9004-2 5.2.3*, which refers to paragraph 5.2.3 of ISO 9004 part 2, or *BS5750 part 4 4.14*, which refers to paragraph 4.14 of BS 5750 part 4.

The most relevant standards are:

* **ISO 9000**: *Quality management and quality assurance standards - Guidelines for selection and use* which is intended to clarify the distinctions and inter-relationships among the principal quality concepts, and provide guidelines for the selection from and use of the rest of the ISO 9000 series

* **BS 5750 Part 4**: *Guide to the use of BS 5750 Part 1, Part 2 and Part 3*, provides guidance to suppliers on how to interpret and apply the chosen standard, it is intended to provide a better understanding of the models and to assist in their use, either in implementing or evaluating a quality system (the ISO equivalent **ISO 9000-2** is not yet published)

* **ISO 9001**, *Quality systems - Model for quality assurance in design/development, production installation and servicing*. ISO 9001 specifies the requirements for a quality system for a supplier with the capability to design, develop and deliver a service. The requirements set out are aimed at the prevention or early detection of errors during all stages of the service lifecycle. If no service design activities take place within an IT Services organization then **ISO 9002** *Quality systems - Model for quality assurance in production and installation* will be more relevant, and the guidance in this module - restricted as appropriate - may still be applied. **ISO 9003**, *Quality systems - Model for quality assurance in final inspection and test* is not considered to be an appropriate model for quality management for IT Services

* **ISO 9004**, *Quality management and quality system elements - Guidelines* which describes a basic set of elements by which a quality management system can be developed and implemented

* **ISO 9004-2**, *Quality systems - Guide to quality management and quality system elements for services* which gives guidance on establishing and implementing a quality management system for service organizations.

Other relevant International and British standards are listed in Annex B together with a table showing the relevant version (year) and the relationship between the ISO, British Standards Institute, and European numbers for each of the standards referred to here and in the Annex.

Section 2
Introduction

PRINCE

The planning, development and implementation of a QMS should be carried out as a formally defined and managed project or programme of projects. PRINCE is the recommended project management method for central government projects in this area.

SSADM

SSADM (Structured Systems Analysis and Design Method), is the recommended Government method for systems analysis, specification and design. It can be used, if desired, to help to analyze and specify the requirements for a comprehensive IT Services Management System. Examples of SSADM used for this purpose are given in the *IT Infrastructure Support Tools* module of the CCTA Appraisal and Evaluation Library.

The IT Infrastructure Library
Quality Management for IT Services

Section 3
Planning for IT Services quality management

3. Planning for IT Services quality management

This section gives guidance on the planning required to prepare for the development and implementation of a quality management system (QMS) for IT Services. In particular, it addresses planning for an ISO 9001 conformant QMS.

Annex C describes some of the fundamental quality concepts relating to a quality management system for IT Services and relevant IT service concepts. Relevant quality initiatives the Citizen's Charter (Cm 1599), Competing for Quality (Cm 1730), the TickIT Project and Vision 2000 are described in Annex D.

3.1 Procedures

To introduce an ISO 9001 conformant quality system for IT Services may require that a significant programme of activities is carried out. The programme may involve everything required to establish a new QMS - from definition of a quality policy to the implementation of new procedures, and the management of a change of culture. However, **it may require only fine tuning of existing policies and operating procedures in order to comply with the requirements of ISO 9001** (for example if the existing service management functions have been implemented using the guidance in the other IT Infrastructure Library modules).

The text of this section assumes that no quality management system for IT Services exists and that no service management functions have been implemented. However, it is also relevant if some or all service management functions have been implemented, with or without IT Infrastructure Library guidance.

If a QMS already exists, then Annexes E and F will help to evaluate whether or not it conforms with the requirements of ISO 9001.

3.1.1 Overview

The size and scope of any quality initiative will depend on the effectiveness of the existing organization, policies, procedures and methods in delivering quality IT services. However, all initiatives can, and should, start from the same point, a decision by the organization to improve the quality of its IT services.

At whatever level the decision is taken - organizational, IS Directorate or IT Services - the total commitment of the top managers involved is vital. Without this commitment the chances of the desired culture being instilled, and the intended policies and procedures being implemented successfully are small.

The activities to be carried out to plan for quality management of IT Services are:

* appoint an *executive sponsor* - a senior manager who will be responsible for the success of the quality initiative (see 3.1.2)

* conduct a feasibility study to determine, in outline, what must be done and to show that it will benefit the organization (3.1.3)

* decide the scope of the quality initiative (3.1.4)

* appoint a Quality Steering Committee to act as the management board for the initiative (3.1.5)

* establish a Quality Manager to plan and control the initiative (3.1.6)

* define IT Services' quality philosophy, policy and goals (3.1.7)

* plan the quality initiative (3.1.8).

3.1.2 Appoint an Executive Sponsor

Once the decision to improve IT service quality has been made the recommended first step is to appoint a senior manager as the *executive sponsor* for the initiative. The role of the Executive Sponsor is to ensure that the quality initiative achieves the expected benefits and that it is completed within the budgeted cost and timescales.

In a programme to implement an ISO 9001 conformant QMS the role of the Executive Sponsor may include the role of "Management representative" required by ISO 9001 4.1.2.3, or this may be part of the role of the Quality Manager. (ISO 9001 4.1.2.3 states that: "The supplier shall appoint a management representative who, irrespective of other responsibilities, shall have defined authority and responsibility for ensuring that the requirements of this International Standard are implemented and maintained.")

The choice of Executive Sponsor is important since it will signal to all IT Services managers and staff how serious the organization is about the initiative. Whoever undertakes this role should be as senior as the scope of the initiative

Section 3
Planning for IT Services quality management

will allow. For example, if the initiative is restricted to IT Services, then the sponsor could be the IS Director (who is ultimately responsible for the quality of IT services) or the IT Services Manager.

Section 3.3 of this module and the QMS Implementation volume of the QML give more detail on the role, and attributes required, of the Executive Sponsor.

3.1.3 Conduct a feasibility study

The first task of the Executive Sponsor is to commission (or possibly carry out) a short study to determine the requirements for, and feasibility of, an initiative to improve IT service quality.

In general, the feasibility study will be a short review intended only to make an initial assessment of current IT service quality and the costs and benefits of introducing quality management. In particular, it is intended to provide sufficient data to:

* demonstrate to those responsible for funding and supporting the initiative that it will be of benefit; in particular that IT service provision will be cheaper (when all costs of poor quality services are taken into account) and the services themselves more efficient and effective

* allow the study team to assist the Executive Sponsor to plan the next steps to be taken.

However, if the organization as a whole is already convinced of the need for quality management and a QMS then the scope of the feasibility study could be restricted to providing sufficient detail to estimate the likely costs of, and to plan, a quality initiative for IT Services.

Feasibility study objectives

The study should:

* determine the effectiveness of the existing organization, policies, procedures and methods in delivering quality IT services (this will include a comparison against the requirements of ISO 9001, and guidance on this is given in Annexes E and F).

* estimate the costs of quality being incurred by the organization and its customers (that is, the cost of prevention, appraisal, internal failure and external failure - see Annex C Concepts, and section 6)

* identify the extent of any changes required to deliver quality services, estimate the likely costs and potential benefits of making them

* recommend a way forward.

Even if it is intended that the scope of the initiative should be restricted to IT Services the feasibility study should cover not only IT Services, but also any in-house IS strategy, development and maintenance organizations.

The reason for the wide scope of the study is that the purpose of the programme is to improve service quality. This means that the review should ideally consider all aspects of service specification, design, development, implementation, delivery, support and maintenance, so that at the very least:

* the interfaces between IT Services and the other activities can be identified, defined and agreed

* aspects of service quality outside IT Services' control are identified and quality management system elements put in place to prevent problems being introduced to IT Services (for example operational testing of new or modified application systems).

The relationships which should exist between Applications Development, Applications Maintenance and IT Services are discussed in more detail in Annex C.2 (IT service concepts), **Software Lifecycle Support** and **Testing an IT Service for Operational Use**. The links between IT Services and IS Planning are discussed in **Planning and Control for IT Services**.

The feasibility study can be carried out in four stages:

* a review of current strategies and policies

* an examination of IT Services' organization and activities

* a review of IT services from a business and customer viewpoint

* finalisation of the feasibility study report.

Each of these is discussed below. (A principal objective during each of the first three stages is to identify and, wherever possible, quantify the current costs of quality, and to estimate the potential benefits of a QMS.)

Section 3
Planning for IT Services quality management

Review of current strategies and policies

The review of the effectiveness of the existing organization (policies, procedures, methods) should begin with a review of current strategies and policies (see *Appraisal and Evaluation of IS Strategy*, a CCTA IS planning subject guide and CCTA IS Guide A2, *Strategic Planning for Information Systems* for guidance). This will ensure that the feasibility study team has a sound understanding of the organization, the functions it should be performing and the issues facing it in order to judge current performance. The feasibility study team should refer to any available statements of organizational policy or strategy, and the reports and products of any other recent studies and audits of IT Services. It should also examine IT Services' policy, standards and procedure manuals, and any descriptions of the IT services which are available.

IS planners and IT Services managers should be interviewed to assess how IT Services planning is carried out and evaluate the overall strategy for the acquisition and use of IT Services resources. This would include assessing the means by which IT service requirements are identified and how service development priorities are assigned.

Review of IT Services organization and activities

The second stage of the feasibility study should be an examination of IT Services organization and activities. The study team should interview managers and staff, and review plans and records. This will help the feasibility study team to assess:

* how well the IT services resources are managed, deployed, trained and administered

* how effectively the infrastructure is being managed

* how well IT Services design, development, implementation, delivery and maintenance are planned and controlled

* the degree of understanding of quality issues and the level of commitment to quality within IT Services.

(Examples of issues to address are given in Figure 1 overleaf.)

Review of IT services

The third stage of the feasibility study should be a review of IT services to assess the extent to which they meet the requirements of the business and the customers. This need not be a review of all existing services, but a representative sample should be taken. The services to be reviewed should be determined during the first two stages of the feasibility study.

The IT Infrastructure Library
Quality Management for IT Services

Does the organization have a quality policy? If so, are all staff and managers aware of it? Does it appear to be put into practice in day-to-day activities? Does a quality management system exist? Is it documented? Do IT Services staff follow the documented system? Is it effective in maintaining and improving service quality? How can this be demonstrated? Is management and staff responsibility and authority for IT service clearly defined? How do the various activities carried out compare with the best practice described in the relevant IT Infrastructure Library modules?

Do Service Level Agreements exist? If so, do they cover all the areas they should and are they detailed enough? How are service levels agreed? Does IT Services ensure that the requirements are adequately defined and documented? How? Does IT Services ensure that the requirements can be met? How?

How are new services designed? How are the design activities controlled to ensure that the specified requirements are met? Does the service design include: the identification of service characteristics subject to customer evaluation and a standard of acceptability for each; production of a service delivery specification including service delivery characteristics which affect service performance, a standard of acceptability for each, service delivery procedures, service resource requirements (including sub-contractor requirements); a service quality control specification? Does service design include capacity, availability and performance planning? If so how well is this done (are actual levels compared with planned and forecast levels?) Are there any capacity, performance or availability problems? If so, why? What is being done to resolve them, and to ensure that they do not recur?

How are changes to services (including new service introduction) controlled? Does a configuration management system exist? How effective is it at controlling change? What verification and validation (V&V) activities take place? How are V&V requirements identified? Are adequate resources and personnel available for V&V? What is the cost of V&V activities? Can this be considered to be value for money? Why?

How does IT Services ensure that the products and services it purchases will meet the requirements? What purchasing documents are produced? What information do they contain? What V&V of purchased products takes place? How are sub-contracted services assessed? How are relationships with sub-contracted suppliers managed?

How is service delivery controlled? Have critical processes been identified? How is performance against Service Level Agreements (SLAs) measured? What inspection or testing takes place? Are customer views on the services actively sought? What happens once views have been established? How can customers report service incidents? Are reported incidents recorded and classified? How effective is the incident control system? How can this be demonstrated? Do procedures and resources exist for the identification and resolution of problems? Are they effective? How can this be demonstrated? (What are the typical causes of incidents and problems? Are they recurring? Do they occur across several services?) What actions are taken to prevent problem recurrence? What is the cost to IT Services and customers of incidents and problems?

What inspection, measuring and test equipment exists ("equipment" in this context includes software, operations tests – ie system, installation and acceptance tests – and checklists as well as hardware)? How is this calibrated and verified?

What training is carried out? Is it relevant and effective? How can this be demonstrated? How are training needs are identified? Are training records maintained?

What customer liaison activities take place? What is their objective? Are they effective? How can they be demonstrated?

Figure 1: Examples of issues for the IT Services Organization review

Section 3
Planning for IT Services quality management

A major objective of this stage is to obtain the customer view of current IT services and the current IT infrastructure, in particular:

* the perceived levels of service

* any problems encountered with services or the infrastructure and their effect on business operations (wherever possible, the effect should be quantified in money terms)

* which aspects of the current services or the infrastructure users feel should be retained or changed in order to provide the required levels of service.

Examples of areas to address when seeking customer views of services are given in Figure 2.

The feasibility study report

The final stage of the feasibility study should be the preparation of a report setting out the study findings and conclusions, and recommendations for improvements. Wherever possible, the costs of quality (that is, service failure costs and prevention and appraisal costs - see section 6 and Annex C) should be identified or estimated, as should the likely costs of a quality initiative and the potential benefits of a QMS. These should be presented in the form of an outline investment appraisal (see CCTA IS Guide B4: Appraising Investment in Information Systems for guidance on investment appraisal).

How do customers regard the services they receive? Are the actual levels of service received those which are really required? If not, are the actual levels better or worse than required? What problems are there with IT services or their provision? What do they think is the cause? How could the problems be resolved? What is the effect of any problems identified on business operations? Quantify this in money terms if possible.

How do the customers regard any Service Level Agreements which might be in place (eg as a bureaucratic requirement of IT Services, meaningless pieces of paper, a useful definition of agreed service levels, out of date)?

Do the customers use IT services from other suppliers? If so, why? How do they compare?

(See the Customer Liaison module for more guidance on obtaining the views of customers.)

Figure 2: Issues to address when seeking customer views

See Chapter 11 of the QMS Implementation volume of the QML: Quality Costing, for general guidance; and section 6 of this module for a discussion on the costs and benefits of a QMS for IT Services.

3.1.4 Decide the scope of the Quality Initiative

A QMS for IT Services may be developed as part of an organization-wide initiative, as part of an IS Directorate-wide initiative or for IT Services alone. The first of these is the preferred option; the third the least desirable, but possibly the most likely, particularly if IT Services are being considered for market testing or outsourcing. However, there may be benefits from implementing the QMS first in a smaller self-contained unit; for example, it is likely to be easier to obtain commitment.

Senior management must decide on the scope, scale and management of any quality initiative based on results and recommendations of the feasibility study (see 3.1.3). For example:

* should there be a single quality initiative for Applications Development, IT Services and Applications Maintenance, or should these be treated as separate (related or unrelated) initiatives?

* within IT Services should the initiative be carried out across all functions at once or should it be phased? (See section 3.4 Timing for a discussion on this)

* can some functions be omitted from the initiative because they are already operating documented policies and procedures which comply with ISO 9001 requirements?

* Who should be a member of the Quality Steering Committee (see below)?

Note that this IT Infrastructure Library module covers only IT Services. That is, it specifically excludes the QMS requirements for IS planning, application system development, application system maintenance and user training in the use of new IT services. (See the CCTA Quality Management Library for more information on QMS requirements for these areas.)

3.1.5 Establish the Quality Steering Committee

The purpose of the Quality Steering Committee (QSC) is to act as a management board for the introduction, development and implementation of the quality initiative.

If the Quality Steering Committee decides to implement a single quality improvement project to establish a quality management system and the project is to be run using the PRINCE project management methodology, then the QSC may be synonymous with the PRINCE Project Board.

If the QSC decides on several projects then it may choose to consider itself as a Programme Board and establish subsidiary Project Boards for individual projects. (A programme is a group of projects that are managed in a coordinated way to gain benefits over and above those which would be achieved if the projects were to be managed independently).

Membership of the QSC will depend on the scope of the quality initiative, but is likely to include:

* Executive Sponsor
* IS Director
* IT Services Manager
* Quality Manager
* managers of other IT service management functions
* Training Manager
* staff and customer representatives.

3.1.6 Appoint a Quality Manager

Even if the IT Services quality initiative is part of a wider programme for the whole organization, a Quality Manager should be appointed either for the IS Directorate or for IT Services as appropriate (An explanation and diagrammatical representation of how the role can fit into an organization is given in section 3.3.1).

The Quality Manager may be the programme/project manager for QMS implementation, and will be responsible for ensuring compliance to the requirements of the QMS thereafter. In particular the Quality Manager will be responsible for the internal audit programme, quality improvement programmes and quality assurance thereafter.

The Quality Manager will probably have delegated authority from the Executive Sponsor to act as management representative for ISO 9001 purposes (see Annex E.1.2.3) during QMS development and implementation or may become the management representative once the initial programme is complete.

It may be desirable for the Quality Manager to attend training courses on quality concepts and quality system auditing before proceeding with the initiative.

3.1.7 Define IT Services quality philosophy, policies and goals

The first task of the QSC, and in particular the Quality Manager and IT Services Manager, will be to define the quality philosophy, policy and goals for IT Services.

If the IT Services quality initiative is taking place as part of a corporate quality initiative then a corporate quality philosophy and associated policies and goals should already have been defined. The IT Services quality philosophy and policies must be consistent with corporate and IS Directorate philosophies and policies if these exist (and with other corporate or IS Directorate policies - for example purchasing or personnel policies). In this case the QSC will be interpreting the corporate philosophy and policies for use within IT Services and defining IT Services-specific goals which support the corporate goals.

Ideally, even if the IT Services quality initiative is being taken in isolation or as a pilot project, a corporate philosophy, policies and goals should still be set by senior management, and interpreted by the QSC for application to IT Services.

Quality philosophy

A quality philosophy is a statement of a common purpose, shared beliefs and values.

Organizations embracing a quality philosophy need to communicate it clearly to all personnel by means of a vision statement. This vision statement provides a common understanding of the quality ethos required in the organization, and the role that quality will play in future business opportunities and customer satisfaction.

An IT Services quality philosophy might be, for example:

"It is our aim to provide quality IT services, efficiently and cost effectively. This means that we must ensure that our services meet, and continue to meet, customer needs and expectations, and that we must strive continually to

Section 3
Planning for IT Services quality management

improve the way we carry out our service design, development, implementation, delivery, support and maintenance activities. We recognise that in order to achieve this, we must commit to training and developing our staff and continually monitoring and measuring our success in achieving our quality targets."

Quality policy

ISO 8402, 3.4 defines quality policy as "The overall quality intentions and direction of an organization as regards quality, as formally expressed by top management".

The quality policy translates the quality philosophy into core principles of management.

From the IT service perspective the policy should interpret any corporate quality policy and relate it to IT Services own purpose and management objectives.

For a quality policy to be effective it must be authorised by top management and must be clearly defined, understood, implemented and maintained by all staff at all levels.

Quality policy is generally documented at two levels: a general statement of policy, and a point-by-point response to each of the requirements of ISO 9001.

Quality goals

IT Services' quality policy should be translated into the goals it seeks to achieve for its services. Quality goals will typically include objectives such as:

* an increase in the availability of service A to x% by a given date

* a reduction of y% in customer complaints within [number] months

* a z% reduction in operating costs for this year when compared to last.

However, when setting quality objectives a balance needs to be made between the associated costs and the requirement to meet customer needs. For example, an improvement in the availability of an IT service from 95% to 98% may be cost justifiable. Further improvement to 99% may be desired by the customer, but not be required by the business; it may also be very expensive.

3.1.8 Plan the Quality Initiative

Terms of Reference for the initiative

Once the statements of IT Services' quality philosophy, policy and goals have been defined, the QSC should set the terms of reference for the quality improvement programme/project and appoint a programme/project manager.

The project manager's first task - assisted by the IT Service managers - will be to define the products of the project. The products defined should include not only the quality system documentation but also products concerned with the management or quality assurance of the project. Each product description will include the quality criteria that will apply. (See Figure 3 for a list of the major project products.)

Once the product descriptions have been prepared the project manager can prepare a product breakdown structure (PBS), the project initiation document (PID) and the project technical, resource and quality plans.

There will be four major stages to the Quality Initiative:

* Initiation
* Analysis of QMS requirements
* Development of the QMS
* Installation of the QMS.

Each of these stages is described in more detail in section 4. (Figure 4 overleaf shows how these stages map on to the phases defined in the QMS Implementation volume of the QML.)

These four stages of the original quality initiative will be followed by a project evaluation review and a post-implementation review, and by an ongoing cycle of review and improvement, which may include specific quality improvement programmes (QIPs). The initial project needs to set up the organization and procedures for this on-going process.

Ongoing quality improvement is covered in section 5, Post implementation and audit.

At the start of the initiative, only Stages 1 and 2 - initiation and analysis of requirements - should be planned in detail. Detailed plans for stages 3 and 4 - development and installation - will be prepared at the end of Stage 2.

Section 3
Planning for IT Services quality management

Note that the products shown below have been classified according to PRINCE terminology. Management products are products developed and used to manage the project, quality products are those developed and used to assure project quality and technical products are the desired products of the project.

MANAGEMENT PRODUCTS

Feasibility study report
- Current strategies and policies
- IT Services organization & activities
- Current IT Services

Quality initiative scope

Terms of reference

Project initiation document

Plans
- Project plans
  * Product breakdown structure
  * Product descriptions
  * Project technical plan
  * Project resource plan
  * Project quality plan
- Stage plans
- Progress reports

Documentation standards

Project evaluation report

Post-implementation review report

QUALITY PRODUCTS

Quality reviews

Quality audits

Configuration audits

Change requests

TECHNICAL PRODUCTS

Quality philosophy

Quality policy

Quality goals/objectives

Quality awareness exercise

Analysis of QMS requirements

Quality policies and procedures
- Quality manual
- IT Services standards and procedures
- Functional and service standards and procedures

Reviewed Service Level Agreements

Service quality plans

Quality management tools

Training needs analysis

Internal audit programme and schedule of management reviews

Trained IT Services staff

Quality office
- Organization
- Mission and objectives
- Levels of authority
- Staff and other resources

Internal quality auditors

Figure 3: Major quality initiative products

Project or Programme?	Small organizations may be able to run the quality initiative as a single PRINCE project. Large organizations may need to run the initiative as a programme with several different projects - for example, one to define the structure of the quality manual and the interfaces between functions, followed by one project for each Service Management function or group of related functions.
	External assistance may be needed to help to develop the QMS. Guidance on the selection of consultants for system definition is given in the QMS Implementation volume of the QML.
Management of change	The quality initiative is as much about changing the culture of the organization as about developing and introducing new or revised standards and procedures. The management of the culture change should be planned as carefully as the development of the QMS. (See the Quality Training volume of the QML for more information on the development of a quality culture.)
Plan for reviews and audits	Plans for the installation stage should include a programme of internal quality audits and management reviews to establish the effectiveness of the QMS and conformity with its requirements. A programme of internal audits and management reviews will also form a part of the established QMS.
Plan for short-term improvements	The plans for development and installation stages of the initiative should take into account the possibility of making short-term improvements.
Plan for project evaluation	The implementation plans should include a scheduled and resourced project evaluation review at the end of the initiative (see section 5.1.1).
Plan a post-implementation review	Similarly, a formal post-implementation review should be planned for six to twelve months after the full quality management system is in operation (see section 5.1.2).
Planning for ISO 9001 certification	If it is intended to seek ISO 9001 certification, this should be planned. Consideration should be given to:

* the reasons for seeking certification - a business case should be made and approved by top management (section 5.1.10 sets out some of the benefits of certification)

* which accredited certification body will be asked to assess and certify the QMS (see Annex G for an explanation of the role of accreditation and certification bodies and the process of assessment) - the selection of a certification body should be through a competitive tender process.

Section 3
Planning for IT Services quality management

QML model	ITIL model (Quality Management for IT Services module)
Preparation: corporate philosophy, policy & goals	Preparation: corporate philosophy, policy & goals
PHASE 1: Defining the QMS 1100 Appoint Executive Sponsor	**CHAPTER 3: PLANNING FOR IT SERVICES QUALITY MANAGEMENT** Appoint Executive Sponsor
1200 Feasibility study	Feasibility study Initiative scope
1300 Quality steering committee	Quality steering committee
1400 Quality Office	Quality manager/Programme manager (Development team and/or Quality office)
1500 Plan quality initiative	IT Services quality philosophy, policy & goals Plan initiative
1600 Select consultants	Procure consultants if required
1700 Quality awareness seminars	**CHAPTER 4 IMPLEMENTATION** **Stage 1 Initiation** Establish implementation team Train the team Quality awareness exercise
1800 Pre-implementation review (analysis & definition)	**Stage 2 Analysis of QMS requirements**
PHASE 2 Establishing the QMS 2100 Quality training — Define & develop training programme 2200 Quality infrastructure — Costs programme, Change management, Quality audit 2300 QMS framework — Quality manual, Practices manual, Project/contract requirements	**Stage 3 Development of the QMS** Quality policies and procedures Service quality plans Quality management tools Analyze training needs, develop training programme Internal audit programme Plan for ISO 9001 certification **Stage 4 Installation** Staff training Trial run Modify QMS "Go live"
PHASE 3 Review and Improvement	**CHAPTER 5: POST- IMPLEMENTATION AND AUDIT** Project evaluation review Operating the QMS - following procedures (ISO 9001 certification if desired) Post-implementation review On-going review and improvement - review/analysis of performance against targets & quality indicators - problem analysis and correction/prevention - audits & management reviews - quality improvement programmes - staff/management suggestion On-going training

Figure 4: Comparison of QML and IT Infrastructure Library structures

The certification assessment should take place after the QMS has been successfully implemented.

3.2 Dependencies

Three things are required if a successful quality initiative is to be planned:

* a committed and effective Executive Sponsor (see 3.1.2 and 3.3.2.1)

* the resources to carry out the feasibility study and plan the initiative; that is, the people and tools and the funding for them if necessary

* a committed IT Services management team (although it may be that this can only be achieved following the feasibility study) which is prepared to allocate management and staff time and funds to the initiative.

The quality management system development and implementation team should ideally be provided with appropriate software tools to enable them to document, and then easily modify, policies, procedures and standards (although they should be subject to configuration and change management).

3.3 People

3.3.1 Organization

If the quality management system is to be developed for the IS Directorate the Quality Manager should report direct to the IS Director. If the system is restricted to IT Services, then the Quality Manager should report to the IT Services Manager (see Figure 5).

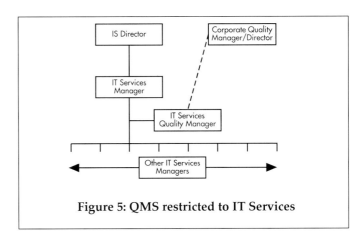

Figure 5: QMS restricted to IT Services

Section 3
Planning for IT Services quality management

If the IS Directorate/IT Services QMS is being established as part of a wider organizational initiative then the ISD/ITS Quality Manager will have a functional reporting line to the organization's Quality Manager (see Figure 6).

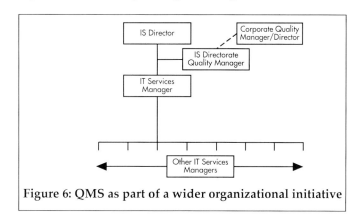

Figure 6: QMS as part of a wider organizational initiative

Small organizations may choose to combine the Quality Management role with another IT Infrastructure Library role.

(A model quality organization for an IS Directorate-wide QMS is given in the QMS Implementation volume of the QML.)

Whatever level is associated with the role the Quality Manager must have the authority to ensure that the requirements of the quality management system are complied with.

It is important to recognise that whatever his or her authority, the Quality Manager alone cannot control the management of IT service quality. Service quality is dependent on, and is the responsibility of, all those involved in service specification, design, development, implementation, delivery, maintenance and improvement. This includes application system developers and maintainers, and customers involved in specification, as well as all IT Services staff. In particular, the managers of service management functions are responsible for the quality of activities carried out in their sections. Overall responsibility for quality lies with the most senior manager in the organization.

3.3.1.1 Quality office

Either before or during the development stage (Stage 3, see 4.1.3), the Quality Steering Committee should consider the staffing requirements for a quality office (often known as "quality assurance", "the quality department" or "the quality management section"). The quality office will be required to assist the Quality Manager to ensure that the requirements of the quality management system are being met and to maintain the QMS and its documentation.

The activities which will be carried out by the quality office will include:

* auditing compliance with the QMS

* monitoring quality trends and customer complaints and the effectiveness of the QMS

* advising IT Services personnel on the quality management system and quality improvement

* planning and assisting with quality improvement programmes

* contributing to management reviews.

The QMS Implementation volume of the QML provides more detail on the role of the quality office.

The size of the quality office will depend on the size of the organization. The QSC should consider whether it needs to be staffed full-time, part-time or by a mix of full and part-time staff.

A large IT Services organization is likely to have several full-time staff to perform internal audits; perhaps supplemented by other IT Services or suitably qualified and trained external staff (eg from application systems development, internal or computer audit or O&M).

In a small IT Services organization, staff may have to perform several roles.

The quality office should report to the Quality Manager.

3.3.1.2 Quality coordinators

In a large IT Services organization it may be desirable to appoint a *quality coordinator* within each IT Services section/function who will be responsible for the functional standards and procedures used by the section. The quality coordinator can also act as a guide for internal and external quality management system auditors during audits, reviews, assessments and surveillance visits, and, if trained as a quality management system auditor could also conduct or assist with internal audits of other IT Services sections or functions. The role of quality coordinator should be combined with another role or roles.

3.3.1.3 Quality councils

For a geographically distributed IT Services organization it may be desirable to establish a *quality council* at each site to coordinate the planning, development and installation of the QMS at that site. (See the QMS Implementation volume of the QML.)

3.3.1.4 Job descriptions

All IT Services personnel perform tasks which affect the quality of services, and so job descriptions should be prepared which set out the responsibilities and authority of each post in relation to quality (see Annex E.1.2.1 and ISO 9001 4.1.2.1).

3.3.2 Staffing

3.3.2.1 Executive Sponsor

The credibility of the quality initiative will depend on the choice of Executive Sponsor. The Executive Sponsor must be committed to improving the quality of IT services, and to command the respect of IT Service managers and staff.

The grade of the Executive Sponsor will depend on the size and nature of the quality initiative but is likely to be Grade 3 to 6 in central Government departments.

The Executive Sponsor should have an understanding of quality concepts and in particular, the costs of quality. This may be obtained from attendance on an appropriate training course or from reading this IT Infrastructure Library module and/or the Quality Management Library.

3.3.2.2 Feasibility study team/individual

The feasibility study may be carried out by a team or an individual. The individual, or the members of the feasibility study team collectively, should have:

* knowledge of IT Service management (ideally at least one member of the team should possess the Information Systems Examination Board (ISEB) Certificate of Proficiency in IT Infrastructure Management (Service Management))

* knowledge of quality management in general, and of the requirements of ISO 9001 and ISO 9004-2 in particular

- experience of conducting feasibility studies (including cost/benefit analysis and investment appraisal)
- knowledge of quality management system assessment
- knowledge of IT effectiveness reviews.

If the study is to cover applications development and maintenance as well as IT Services, then the team should also have systems development and project management experience.

If there is no clearly defined IS strategy, then the team should also have experience of developing IS strategies in order to be able to assess the IT services in terms of the business strategy as well as the customer views which will be sought during the study.

The feasibility study team may be composed of IT Services staff, experienced staff from elsewhere within the IS Directorate or wider organization, consultants or a mixture of the three. If the study is to be carried out by internal staff alone then they should be trained in quality management system review, in planning quality improvement programmes and, if necessary, in the conduct of feasibility studies.

If there is a degree of urgency about the initiative (and the time required to train IT Services staff is not available) then involving experienced staff from outside IT Services, or using consultants, will complement the detailed knowledge of the IT Services staff to be involved, and will add a degree of independence to the review.

3.3.2.3 Quality Manager

The role of the IS Directorate/IT Quality Manager (referred to in this module as the Quality Manager) is to:

- bring about and maintain a change in IT Services' culture to ensure the delivery of quality IT services
- ensure that the requirements of the quality management system are being met
- maintain the QMS and its documentation (this will include preparing and resourcing an internal quality audit programme and a series of management reviews).

A more detailed list of the tasks to be undertaken by the Quality Manager is given in Figure 7.

Section 3
Planning for IT Services quality management

The IT Services Quality Manager's primary goal is to integrate quality into all of IT Services' business functions. The Quality Manager must also ensure that the provision of products and services meets the quality requirements of the customer.

The responsibilities of the Quality Manager include the following tasks:

- assist the QSC to define IT Services' quality philosophy, policies and goals

- produce and manage the project plans for the implementation of the QMS

- undertake quality reviews/audits to assess improvements to meet business and customer needs

- manage the production of quality policies and procedures manuals for IT Services and advise IT Services managers and staff on the development of ISO 9001 conformant systems

- initiate and manage a quality awareness, education and improvement programme; develop a trained and motivated quality team

- manage the development of quality plans for existing and new IT Services

- ensure that the QMS meets the requirements of ISO 9001

- set and monitor performance criteria for the QMS and the quality office

- identify business and customer related improvements from quality audit, staff suggestion schemes, customer questionnaires and other sources; where appropriate prepare investment appraisals and business cases for quality improvements

- report on the effectiveness and efficiency of the QMS to IT Services Management, the QSC and the Executive Sponsor

- liaise with certification bodies, customers and suppliers on quality issues

- coordinate with safety/legal representatives, etc on product safety and service liability where appropriate.

Based on section 6.9.3 'The Quality Manager' of the QMS Implementation volume of the QML.

Figure 7: Tasks for the Quality Manager

The role of the Quality Manager is likely to be full-time during the initial quality initiative. Once the QMS has been installed and is functioning effectively then, depending on the size of the organization, it may be possible to combine it with other roles and responsibilities. However, it is important that there should be no conflict of interest.

On this basis the best candidates for combining roles are Customer Liaison Manager or Configuration Manager.

The Quality Manager plays a key role within the quality initiative. It is important that the role is filled by someone with appropriate experience, skills and qualities. Ideally the Quality Manager should possess:

* a thorough understanding of IT Services'/IS Directorate's business, IS, IT and management strategies and policies

* an understanding of the businesses, strategies and policies of customers and suppliers

* knowledge and experience of business, IT Services and project management (ideally using PRINCE)

* the capacity for lateral thinking, imagination and vision

* communication and presentation skills

* a flexible but decisive management style

* analytical and problem solving skills

* leadership skills, including the ability to motivate staff

* general tenacity in pursuing quality objectives.

On appointment the Quality Manager should undertake any education and training necessary to obtain the necessary knowledge, skills and capabilities.

The Quality Manager should be encouraged to work towards professional and other appropriate qualifications in quality and IT service management. These may include qualification as a quality auditor, relevant National Vocational Qualifications, and the ISEB Certificates of Proficiency in IT Infrastructure Management (Service Management) and Project Management (PRINCE).

Section 3
Planning for IT Services quality management

3.3.2.4 QMS Programme/Project Managers

Ideally, the Quality Manager will manage the QMS implementation team (see 3.3.2.5). However, it may be necessary or desirable to employ a separate programme or project manager (see 3.1.8) for this role:

* the QSC may consider that no one individual is available with the skills to undertake both the Quality Manager and Project/Programme Manager roles and so may appoint one person to manage the QMS implementation, and one to manage the quality office and on-going quality improvement

* the QSC may consider that appointing a separate project manager for the quality initiative would emphasise that the initiative and resulting QMS is not just the property of the Quality Office, but the whole of the IS Directorate or IT Services (in this case the Quality Manager may take on the PRINCE project board Senior Technical role).

If a separate Programme/Project Manager for the initiative is to be appointed then ideally he or she should possess the ISEB certificate of proficiency in project management, be trained in the audit of quality management systems and in the management of projects using PRINCE. (If the Programme/Project Manager and Quality Manager roles are to be filled by different persons then the Quality Manager need only be trained in PRINCE at an overview level.)

If the quality initiative is to be run as a programme then the project managers for the development of the QMS might be other IT Services managers. For example, the Configuration Manager could be appointed as project manager for the development of those parts of the QMS dealing with configuration and change management, and the Cost Manager could be responsible for developing the quality costing system (see 4.1.3.1 Quality policies and procedures).

3.3.2.5 QMS implementation team

The QMS implementation team (see 4.1.1.1) will assist the QMS programme/project manager (under the guidance of the Quality Steering Committee) to define, develop and implement the QMS. The team may be formed from the members of the quality office (if it exists - see section 3.4). Alternatively, the team may evolve into (or some members may become, or form the kernel of) the quality office (see 3.3.1.1).

At least some members of the team should be, or be trained as, quality system auditors so that internal audits, reviews and assessments of QMS effectiveness can be carried out during and immediately after the trial run of the QMS.

If quality coordinators (see 3.3.1.2) have been or are to be appointed then they should be members of the team.

3.3.2.6 Internal quality auditors

Personnel who are to perform the role of IT Services internal quality auditors should be trained in quality system audit. ISO 10011-2 sets out qualification criteria for quality systems auditors which include:

* education to at least secondary level

* demonstrated competence in expressing concepts and ideas clearly and fluently both orally and in writing

* training to the extent necessary to ensure their competence in the skills required for carrying out audits (TickIT auditor training - see Annex D - may be particularly relevant for internal auditors of an IT Services QMS; details of the `Requirements of the National Registration Scheme for TickIt Auditors' are available from the Institute of Quality Assurance which operates a national register of auditors for quality systems).

3.3.3 Training

Training for personnel at all levels and in all functions within IT Services is central to the successful functioning of the QMS and the achievement of quality IT services; that is, both specific training to perform assigned tasks and general training to heighten quality awareness and to influence attitudes. The organization must therefore:

* identify the skills, knowledge and qualifications required to carry out tasks

* determine the training needs of the individuals to be assigned to carry out those tasks

* plan and carry out appropriate specific training (this may be provided either internally or externally)

* plan and carry out general quality awareness programmes

> * retain records of education, qualification, skills, training and experience which can be used to help to judge the training requirements of personnel.

Particular attention should be paid to the selection and training of new personnel and of personnel transferred to new assignments.

3.4 Timing

3.4.1 Feasibility study

The four stages of the feasibility study (described in section 3.1.3) can be carried out sequentially or, stage 1 (the review of current strategies and policies) can, if desired, be followed by the other three stages carried out in parallel; this depends on the resources available.

For a large IT Services organization, the feasibility study is likely to take five or six weeks elapsed time for a team of two. For a small organization it will take two to four weeks.

3.4.2 Quality Steering Committee

If desired, the Quality Steering Committee can be established before the appointment of the Executive Sponsor or before the feasibility study is carried out.

3.4.3 Quality Manager

If desired, the Quality Manager may be appointed before the feasibility study is carried out.

3.4.4 Quality goals

Corporate quality goals should be set by senior management when developing the organization's quality philosophy, and general IT Services quality goals which will contribute towards the corporate goals should be set by the QSC at the start of the quality initiative. However, the setting of specific IT service-based (as opposed to the general) quality targets may be left until after the analysis of QMS requirements (4.1.2); and in particular, until after the review of customer satisfaction. It may make sense to leave this until after the preparation of quality plans for existing services (see section 4.1.3.2).

3.4.5 Quality office

The quality office (see 3.3.1.1) may be established at the same time as the Quality Manager is appointed (or shortly afterwards) to assist with the documentation of policies and procedures. If this is the case then the quality office personnel may also be the QMS implementation team or its nucleus.

The IT Infrastructure Library
Quality Management for IT Services

4. Implementation

This section describes the implementation of the IT Services quality management system (QMS).

4.1 Procedures

There are four stages in the implementation of a quality management system:

* Initiation
* Analysis of requirements
* Development of the QMS
* Installation of the QMS.

4.1.1 Stage 1 Initiation

In the initiation stage the project manager will assemble and, if necessary, train the team to develop and install the quality management system, conduct a quality awareness exercise, and establish the controls and systems to manage the initiative.

4.1.1.1 The QMS implementation team

Although a quality management function may be established as part of the initiative, quality management is different from other IT service management functions such as availability management or capacity planning. Quality management must also be *a part of* all IT service management functions. It is about defining how the other functions should be carried out - individually and as a whole - in order to achieve the aim of customer satisfaction, cost effectively.

Ideally, the QMS implementation team should contain members from each of the IT service management functions included within the scope of the initiative, and if possible from differing levels within the organization structure. This approach helps to increase involvement in the initiative and share responsibility. It also helps to spread the workload which will be considerable, especially if no formal quality management system already exists.

4.1.1.2 Train the team

The team should be trained in quality concepts and, ideally, in quality system auditing.

4.1.1.3 Mount a quality awareness exercise

The QMS to be developed will work effectively only if the people involved are committed to IT service quality. Commitment must come first and foremost from the IS Director and IT Services Manager, who must ensure that the managers of each service management function understand the requirement for quality and their responsibility for it. The function managers must in turn brief their staff.

The quality awareness exercise is an important step in the initiative since it will help to bring about the required change in IT Services culture.

As the initiative proceeds, awareness of the importance of quality to IT Services and commitment to it can be reinforced by other components of a quality awareness programme such as further briefings, circulars or newsletters, discussion papers, seminars for interested parties, posters and a project name and logo.

The exercise should introduce quality concepts, such as the cost of quality, and stress the benefits and costs of introducing or improving the quality management function. Use the example benefits described in section 6 of this module. The exercise should also stress the possible problems resulting from the lack of a formal quality management system, wherever possible using examples from the organizations own experience (suitable examples may have been identified during the feasibility study).

It is also important to plan to retain awareness of quality and commitment to it once the quality management system and function are implemented; for example, by means of quality awards and comparisons of achievements against team performance targets.

4.1.1.4 Project control

The project should be managed using a formal methodology such as PRINCE.

It should be noted that since the project is implementing an ISO 9001 conformant QMS, document control procedures (see Annex E.5 and ISO 9001 4.5) will be particularly important.

4.1.2 Stage 2
Analysis of QMS requirements

The second stage of the project is a detailed assessment of where IT Services is now in terms of quality, and what needs to be done to improve quality. It will have the same basic objectives as the feasibility study, but will examine current business objectives, policies, procedures and activities in more detail. (If a detailed assessment was carried out earlier instead of a high level feasibility study, then this stage may be omitted, or may focus on areas that need further in-depth analysis.)

The assessment should compare current policies and practice with the best practice guidance given in the IT Infrastructure Library, and establish the degree of compliance with the requirements of ISO 9001 (guidance on this is given in 3.1.3 and Annexes E and F). The assessment should also include a comprehensive review of customer satisfaction with IT services (see section 3.1.2.3 of the **Customer Liaison** module for guidance on assessing customer satisfaction).

Carrying out the assessment is a major task, and it is important to allow sufficient resource and time to carry it out effectively.

If desired, the existing practices may be analyzed using a structured systems analysis method such as SSADM.

Staff involvement

Wherever possible, IT Services staff should be involved in the analysis of QMS requirements. For example:

* in task forces (led by members of the QMS implementation team) to investigate areas within IT Services identified as requiring further analysis during the feasibility study

* in workshops assessing the effectiveness of existing policies and procedures.

Use of existing procedures and plans

Wherever possible, existing (effective) policies, procedures and quality plans should be used as the basis for the development of the quality management system - there is little or nothing to be gained by changing what already works. Most IT Services organizations are likely to have many of the components for a QMS in place already (for example, change management procedures, operational procedures and procurement procedures), and the assessment should define the improvements necessary to the existing systems and procedures.

Plan for development
and installation

Once the necessary improvements have been identified the team should identify the costs of quality and the project manager should produce detailed plans for development and installation stages of the initiative (see 4.1.3 and 4.1.4 below).

4.1.3 Stage 3 Development of the QMS

The purpose of the third stage of the initiative is to develop the organization structure, policies, procedures, processes and resources, and procure any tools, required for the QMS. The major activities are:

* develop and document detailed quality policies, procedures and standards, including a quality costing system and an internal quality audit system

* develop quality plans for existing services

* specify and procure quality management tools

* analyze IT Services staffing and training needs and, if appropriate, customer training needs; develop an education and training strategy and materials

* prepare an audit programme and schedule management reviews; recruit or train internal auditors if required

* plan for ISO 9001 certification if appropriate.

Staff involvement

Wherever possible, IT Services staff should be involved in the development of the QMS. For example:

* in quality circles or via suggestion schemes, to contribute suggestions on how to improve IT service quality, so that these can be considered for inclusion in the documented QMS

* in developing or refining policies and procedures

* in developing quality plans for existing services

* in the specification and evaluation of service and quality management tools

* to help ensure that policies and procedures are not over specified.

Participation in the development of the QMS will help to engender ownership of the procedures, and stimulate the required culture change. It will also help to ensure that the QMS is not viewed as an imposition by senior management.

Section 4
Implementation

4.1.3.1 Quality policies and procedures

The IT Services quality philosophy and overall quality policy will have been approved by the Quality Steering Committee and ideally by senior management. The analysis of QMS requirements will have identified the areas where more detailed quality policies, and standards and procedures need to be developed and adopted within IT Services.

The quality policies, standards and procedures to be developed should be documented in a systematic and structured manner. Three levels of documentation are normally appropriate to document the IT Services quality management system:

* a statement of detailed quality policies (often known as the *quality manual*)

* IT Services-wide standards and procedures

* functional and service-based standards and procedures.

All these manuals are controlled documents (see Annex E5).

Quality manual

The quality manual serves three purposes:

* first, it needs to set out IT Services' quality policies and procedures for use by IT Services staff (note that procedures will not be defined in the quality manual, rather it will include references to specific procedures manuals or high-level procedures, ie not work instructions)

* second, it is a document which will be read outside IT Services by customers who will be looking for IT Services commitment to satisfying their needs, and by suppliers to IT Services in order to increase their awareness of quality and to help them to meet IT Services requirements; it must therefore be written in a way which can be understood outside IT Services

* third, it may be read by second or third-party auditors to establish the effectiveness of the QMS and its conformance with a particular set of requirements (such as the requirements of ISO 9001); it should, therefore, help them to establish the relationship between the documented policies and procedures and the appropriate requirements (for example, by cross-referencing policy statements to paragraphs of ISO 9001).

The overall structure of the quality manual should be designed principally to meet IT Services needs and should fit the culture and style of the organization.

Annex E gives guidance on the policies required.

The quality manual should include a definition of:

* the organizational structure and responsibilities for quality, including a definition of the quality management function (see section 3.3 for more detail on this)

* the technical interfaces between each of the IT Services functions (Annex I gives guidance on the interrelationships between IT Infrastructure Library modules)

* the interfaces with other areas of the organization which can affect or influence IT Service quality; for example, Applications Development, Applications Maintenance, IS Planning and Procurement (see Annex C).

IT Services-wide standards and procedures

Whenever a standard or procedure applies to all, most or even several IT service management functions it should be documented at the IT Services-wide level. There are three reasons for this: to avoid duplication of effort in development and maintenance; to ensure common practices where relevant; and to ensure that an appropriate level of change control is applied.

Topics for which IT Services-wide standards and procedures are appropriate are, for example: service design, the development of Service Level Agreements, the development of service quality plans (see), configuration and change management, document control, quality record keeping, quality costing (see below), service performance analysis and improvement, quality improvement programmes (see section 5), purchasing and sub-contractor assessment, complaints, and the use of standards or methodologies such as PRINCE and SSADM.

Functional and service-based standards and procedures

Functional and service-based standards contain the information required to manage and improve a specific IT service management function or service. They should contain information which is relevant only to that function or service.

Functional standards and procedures

The functional standards and procedures will cover the local operating standards and procedures for each IT service management function (detailed guidance on how to plan for and establish each function is given in sections 3 and 4 of

Section 4
Implementation

the relevant IT Infrastructure Library module; Annex F provides detailed guidance on the application of ISO 9001 to each IT service management function).

It is worth remembering that in some cases - principally for those functions whose remit extends across IT Services - procedures and standards must be defined at both the functional and IT Services-wide levels. For example, the functional standards and procedures to be developed will include local standards and procedures for the *management and improvement* of the Configuration Management *function*. The IT Services-wide standards and procedures will include the configuration and change management standards and procedures which apply to all IT Services staff.

Ideally, these common standards and procedures should be identified before the development of individual functional and service-based standards and procedures begins, in order to avoid unnecessary duplication.

Service-based standards and procedures

The specification of requirements for an IT service (see Annex C.1.1) must be translated into bespoke and/or packaged application software (outside the scope of this module) and into a service delivery specification and Service quality control specifications and a Service Level Agreement or agreements.

The service delivery specification will comprise:

* service delivery procedures (comprising service-specific operations standards and procedures)

* service resource requirements; that is, requirements for things such as equipment, software, personnel (roles, skills and numbers), sub-contractors and consumables

* a contingency plan for the service (or modifications to an organization-wide contingency plan - see **Contingency Planning**.)

The service delivery procedures (and application software) should be designed to allow quality to be measured and controlled. To help to achieve this, a quality control specification should be prepared for the IT service, defining, in addition to customer service characteristics:

* characteristics that may not be observable by the customer, but that directly affect service delivery

* a standard of acceptability for each characteristic

* defined methods for evaluating each characteristic

* where appropriate, defined ways to influence or control the characteristics within specified limits.

The IT service quality control specification will be developed into a service quality plan (see 4.1.3.2).

Each Service Level Agreement (SLA) should include a clear definition of the service characteristics that are observable and subject to customer evaluation - for example, response times and availability - and evaluation criteria, and a charging policy if appropriate (see Annex J for more detail on service quality characteristics, and **Service Level Management** for more guidance on SLAs).

Quality costing system

The cost of IT service quality (see Annex C.1.4) is a vital measure of the effectiveness of the quality management system, and a quality costing system should be developed as part of the QMS and integrated with the IT Services cost management system (see **Cost Management for IT Services**).

The system should cover:

* the quality related costs to be collected and analyzed (examples of quality related costs for IT Services are given in section 6)

* cost and cost trend analysis and reporting

* how quality related costs are to be allocated to cost units (see **Cost Management for IT Services**)

* comparison with other IT Services costs (eg total quality cost against the total cost of IT service provision).

More detail on quality costing is given in the QMS Implementation volume of the QML and on IT services costing in the **Cost Management** volume of the IT Infrastructure Library.

Quality costing procedures and standards should be referred to in IT Services-wide, functional and service-based standards and procedures manuals and documented in service quality plans as appropriate.

It may be desirable to conduct a pilot quality costing system study for a given service as part of the quality initiative in order to determine the best way to obtain the desired costing information.

Quality audit system   The quality audit manual should define:

* the objectives for quality audits and management reviews
* the criteria for selecting areas of IT Services for audit
* standards for audit planning, preparation, conduct and reporting
* audit procedures
* non-conformity follow-up procedures
* quality auditor qualification and training requirements
* performance measures and targets for the audit function.

The internal QMS audit function should be developed to conform to the requirements of ISO 10011, *Guidelines for auditing quality systems* (which comes in three parts - see Annex B). There are two major benefits to this:

* ISO 10011 documents current "best practice" for quality audit and so conforming to its requirements should help to ensure effective quality audit and contribute to the improvement of the QMS
* ISO 9001 certification assessments and surveillance visits (see Annex G) will be carried out by external auditors working to the standards of ISO 10011; internal auditors working to the same model should have discovered and taken corrective action over any actual or potential non-conformities which might have been detected by the external audit.

4.1.3.2 Service quality plans

As part of QMS development a quality plan should be prepared for each existing service and, once the QMS is established, for each new service. A quality plan is a document "setting out the specific quality practices, resources and sequence of activities relevant to a particular ...service..." (ISO 8402, *Quality vocabulary*). To develop quality plans for existing services it will be necessary to:

* review any SLAs and requirements specifications which exist to establish the service requirements
* review existing general operations and service-specific activities and procedures

- identify the key processes or resources which affect the service quality

- analyze those processes and resources to select those characteristics whose measurement and control will ensure service quality (these will include the customer service characteristics)

- determine how to measure, evaluate and influence or control the specified characteristics

- define the quality practices and resources to be applied

- identify any requirements for measurement and evaluation tools.

To implement quality plans for existing services it may be necessary to:

- modify the general operations and service-specific procedures to ensure that the required actions are carried out

- modify applications software, systems software and hardware configurations as appropriate so that the required quality can be measured and achieved.

Care needs to be taken not to raise customer expectations beyond what can be achieved during the review of SLAs and development of service quality plans. It should be made clear that this is the start of a quality improvement process, and that both time and customer cooperation will be required to achieve the objectives.

(Also see the chapter on quality plans in the QMS Implementation volume of the QML.)

4.1.3.3 Specify and procure quality management tools

Effective quality management of IT Services will be assisted by the use of tools (which will mostly be shared with other IT Services functions). The tools required for quality management are discussed in section 7. If these are not already available, then the requirements for them should be specified, the likely costs and benefits established and, if justified, the tools procured as part of the QMS development exercise.

It may help to specify the requirements for quality management tools using structured analysis and specification techniques such as those included in SSADM

(Structured Systems Analysis and Design Method), which will help to identify the requirements for the integration of tools to meet the needs of individual IT Service functions, and IT Services as a whole.

4.1.3.4 Analyze training needs

For quality management to be effective requires not only that staff should be committed to quality, but also that they are capable of carrying out the tasks assigned to them. ISO 9001 requires that personnel performing activities affecting IT Service quality "shall be qualified on the basis of appropriate education, training and/or experience" (ISO 9001, 4.18).

Therefore, once the QMS has been defined (and this should include identification of the skill, knowledge and qualifications required to carry out quality related tasks) then the training needs of the individuals to be assigned to carry out quality related tasks should be identified, and appropriate training planned and provided.

In the case of internal quality audit, in addition to training existing staff as auditors, it may be desirable either to recruit experienced staff to prepare the audit and management review programme and to lead audit teams, or to plan to engage suitably qualified consultants to do so until internal staff have sufficient experience.

Customer education

It may also be desirable to educate customers in various aspects of the QMS (for example in use of the help desk and incident escalation procedures, in the contents and implications of their SLAs), and to (re)train them in the use of the IT services if lack of understanding has been identified as a cause of dissatisfaction or a high number of incidents.

4.1.3.5 Prepare an internal audit programme and schedule management reviews

As part of the development of the audit system, a programme of internal audits and management reviews should be prepared. Internal audits and management reviews are requirements of ISO 9001 – ISO 9001 requires that a comprehensive system of planned and documented internal quality audits is carried out (ISO 9001, 4.17), and that the quality system shall be reviewed at appropriate intervals by the supplier's management to ensure its continuing effectiveness (ISO 9001 4.1.3).

Outline plans for internal audits and management reviews to be carried out during the installation stage of the quality initiative should have been prepared during the analysis of QMS requirements (Stage 2); these should be refined as the development proceeds. The audit programme should ensure that all major functions and types of procedure are covered at least once during an annual cycle.

4.1.3.6 Preparing for ISO 9001 certification

If ISO 9001 certification is to be sought then it may be desirable to engage a lead auditor registered with the Institute of Quality Assurance to review the documented QMS for ISO 9001 compliance. Any recommended additions and changes should be made before installation of the QMS.

4.1.4 Stage 4 Installation of the QMS

The purpose of the installation stage is to introduce and trial the quality management system, and then modify it if necessary. At the end of this stage the QMS should be self-sustaining and improving, and able to adapt to changes in business requirements. The major activities during this stage are:

* set up the quality management function (in particular, QMS audit) if this has not already been done during the initiation, analysis or development stages (see 3.3)

* train staff in the use of the new procedures, and issue manuals and procedures

* trial run the QMS, and carry out the audits and reviews planned earlier

* modify policies and procedures if required, and install the revised QMS

* continue with any education and training programme started in stage 3.

4.1.4.1 Staff training

It is important that all staff are trained in the standards and procedures which apply to their jobs; the training needs to cover not only what should be done but also why. The training should include an overview of the QMS as a whole and an explanation of the quality philosophy and objectives and their rationale - ideally this should be presented by a top management representative such as the Executive Sponsor, the IS Director or the IT Services Manager in order to emphasise the organization's commitment to the QMS.

All staff should be made aware of the benefits of achieving the quality and performance objectives, and of the effects of poor performance on customers and in the medium to long term on IT Services itself.

The training should make it clear that the cost effective provision of quality services is not the responsibility of the quality management function, but of all staff within IS Services.

The training courses should be developed so that they can also be used as part of the induction of new staff, or of staff moving from one function to another.

Where appropriate, customers should also be made aware of the new procedures and how to use them - for example, complaints procedures.

4.1.4.2 Trial run

The initial period of QMS operation should be regarded as a trial run of the new procedures. Staff should be encouraged to examine the operation and documentation of the system critically, and to propose improvements. The quality management function should monitor and audit the operation of the system, propose improvements and provide advice and guidance to staff on the use of the QMS as required.

A major focus during this period should be to ensure that the various sets of procedures provide complete coverage, that the interfaces between them function correctly and that there is no unnecessary duplication. Everyone should also seek to remove any unnecessary requirements from the QMS which may have been included due to excessive zeal during Stage 3 - for example, requirements to complete forms when a freeform note giving specified information would be just as effective. (Note that forms should be controlled documents).

Customers should be made aware that the new policies, procedures and standards are being introduced (they should have been involved in the review of SLAs and development of service quality plans). It is important to manage customer expectations, particularly during the trial period when the new procedures may not function as effectively as desired.

4.1.4.3 Modify the system

Any proposed modifications to the QMS must be subjected to the defined change control procedures.

4.2 Dependencies

Five things are required if a successful quality management system is to be implemented:

* committed senior management; especially the IS Director

* a committed and effective Executive Sponsor

* the resources to analyze the QMS requirements and develop and install the system

* a committed IT Service management team which is prepared to devote management time to the initiative

* committed IT Services staff - a major objective of the quality initiative is to engender staff commitment to the delivery of cost effective, quality IT Services.

The ease of implementation will also be affected by the capacity of the organization to change. Steps should be taken as part of the quality initiative to increase this capacity and this should have been planned (see management of change in section 3.1.8). Capacity to change may also be affected by external factors such as market testing of IT Services.

4.3 People

The QMS implementation programme will be led by staff in the roles identified in section 3.3, but the successful implementation of a QMS for IT Services will require the training, commitment and involvement of all IT Services staff, and the involvement and possibly the training and involvement of customers.

4.4 Timing

Detailed quality policies and objectives for IT Services should be developed first. Then the product descriptions and product breakdown structure prepared by the project manager should be reviewed, and a more detailed specification of the structure and content of the standards and procedures manuals prepared addressing the problems and requirements identified during the analysis stage. These should be reviewed for completeness and consistency. Once this has been done then each part of the

QMS can be developed and implemented as a separate project or sub-project. If sufficient resources are available, then these can be carried out in parallel.

If resource availability requires a phased approach to QMS implementation then the various functions should be implemented in approximately the following order:

* configuration management, change management and software control and distribution, problem management, operations management, network management and quality audit

* help desk, service level management, capacity management, availability management and cost management

* customer liaison, managing supplier relationships, operational testing, contingency planning.

This order may be affected by various business specific requirements. For example, the need to implement a cost management system before the start of the next financial year, or service level management before an outsourcing or market testing exercise.

Within each phase, the functions can be implemented in parallel or broadly in the order shown above.

(Annexes E and F give more detail on which parts of each IT service management function are essential or desirable for an ISO 9001 conformant QMS, and Annex I discusses the interdependencies of the IT service management functions defined in the IT Infrastructure Library.)

4.4.1 Timescales

Guidance on the time required to implement each IT service management function in a "green field" site (that is a new site, or an existing site without formal IT infrastructure management functions in operation) is given in the appropriate IT Infrastructure Library module.

The timescales (and effort) required to implement a QMS will depend on the effectiveness of the current procedures and the degree of conformity with ISO 9000. However, the time required to plan and implement an effective QMS - given the necessary commitment and required resource - is likely to be between 12 and 18 months.

If current procedures comply with or are based on the best practice described in the IT Infrastructure Library, then this timescale may be reduced. For a green field site the exercise could take over two years.

The IT Infrastructure Library
Quality Management for IT Services

Section 5
Post-implementation and audit

5. Post-implementation and audit

5.1 Procedures

The quality management activities which take place once the quality management system has been implemented are:

* a project evaluation review, or reviews (5.1.1)
* a post-implementation review (5.1.2)
* audits and management reviews of the QMS and the quality management section (5.1.3)
* customer contract reviews; that is, reviews of IT Services ability to meet the requirements set out in requirements specifications and SLAs (5.1.4)
* the development and monitoring of quality plans for new services and service design reviews as part of service design (5.1.5)
* service quality monitoring and control (5.1.6)
* configuration management and change control (5.1.7)
* an ongoing cycle of review and improvement of IT services, products and the QMS, which may include specific quality improvement programmes (5.1.8)
* training (5.1.9).

If desired, ISO 9001 certification may be sought from an accredited body following implementation. The merits of certification are discussed in section 5.1.10. The certification process is summarised in Annex G, and described in detail in the QMS Implementation volume of the QML. The timing of certification is discussed in section 5.4.

5.1.1 Project evaluation review

An evaluation review should have been scheduled, during the planning phase (see section 3.1.8), for each project carried out as part of the quality initiative. The objective of the evaluation is to provide an assessment of the management of the project to ensure that the experience gained is documented and used in future projects or quality improvement programmes. It should review:

* actual timescales, resource utilisation and the achievement of milestones against planned
* the effectiveness of the management procedures, tools and processes used

> * any problems encountered by the project and how they were, and with hindsight should have been, resolved.

5.1.2 Post-implementation review

A post-implementation review should have been scheduled during the planning phase of the initiative (see 3.1.8). The objective of the review is to establish the extent to which the objectives of the quality initiative have been met as an input to quality improvement.

5.1.3 Management review and internal quality audit

Management reviews and a programme of internal quality audits addressing all aspects of the QMS are requirements of ISO 9001 (and should be a component of any QMS even if ISO 9001 certification is not to be sought). External audits will be required if ISO 9000 certification is sought, and may also be required by some customers. The various types of audit are described in Annex H.

5.1.3.1 Management review

The purpose of management review of the QMS is to ensure that the system is up-to-date (both in terms of its aim and its implementation), effective and controlled.

IS Directorate or IT Services management, or competent personnel on behalf of management, should carry out periodic reviews of the:

* documented policies, goals and procedures that define the QMS
* results of internal audits
* results of specific quality initiatives
* results of comparisons of customer assessments of service quality (gained by customer satisfaction surveys for example) with internal assessments of service quality
* effectiveness, costs and benefits of the QMS.

(All these factors may, if desired, be addressed in a single review.)

Section 5
Post-implementation and audit

Policies, goals and procedures	Reviews of the documented policies, goals and procedures should determine how closely they reflect the business objectives and working methods of the organization and ensure that they are updated and promulgated as necessary.
Reviews of internal audits	Reviews of internal audit results should ensure that the the defined QMS is implemented as required. The reviews should:

* evaluate the findings of audits and ensure that required corrective actions have been taken
* assess the overall effectiveness of the QMS in achieving its stated objectives
* assess what changes, if any, are necessary
* prioritise any outstanding corrective or preventative action and make resources available
* consider, and where appropriate, approve proposed quality improvement programmes
* assess the effectiveness of the audit programme.

Quality initiatives	The results of quality initiatives (quality improvement programmes) should be determined by project evaluation and post-implementation reviews.
Customer satisfaction	"Customer assessment is the ultimate measure of the quality of a service" (ISO 9004-2). IT Services should institute ongoing assessments and measurements of customer satisfaction. These should be compared with IT Services own assessments of service quality (it is quite possible for an IT Services organization to believe that it is providing a good service, but for the customer to disagree), and the need for any action identified. The action to be taken could, for example, be service quality improvement, customer education or training, or revision of the SLA to clarify the service to be provided.
QMS effectiveness	Management should consider the effectiveness of the QMS in achieving or improving quality goals, targets and agreed service levels and compare this with the costs of quality (see Annex C.1.4).
Management review outcomes	As a result of a management review, quality objectives may be revised; QMS organization, roles, responsibilities or authorities may change; performance measures and quality cost targets may be revised; quality improvement programmes may be started or stopped; or the QMS itself may be modified.

Management review procedures
The procedures for management review should be documented as part of the QMS, and records should be kept of the reviews and any changes made.

5.1.3.2 Internal quality audit

Internal quality audits are carried out to ensure that the defined quality system is being operated correctly and effectively.

A quality audit is defined as a "systematic and independent examination to determine whether quality activities and related results comply with planned arrangements and whether these arrangements are implemented effectively and are suitable to achieve objectives" (ISO 8402).

Two key points to note in this definition are that quality audits should be:

* systematic - they should be carried out in a methodical way; this means that audits should be planned and carried out in a structured way and that individual audits should follow an appropriate *audit strategy*

* independent - they should be carried out by persons who are not directly involved in the function or procedure being audited so that there is no conflict of interests; this is a key requirement of ISO 9001.

Audit objectives
Internal audits should check:

* that the QMS documentation meets the needs of the organization

* that the quality management system meets the requirements of the relevant quality system standard (eg ISO 9001) or contract

* that the requirements of the quality system are being complied with

* that the documented procedures are practical, understood and followed

* whether the quality system is effective in ensuring the maintenance and improvement of quality in services.

Internal auditors should also:

* give guidance on how non-conformities might be corrected

Section 5
Post-implementation and audit

* identify possible improvements to the QMS which will lead to increases in cost-effectiveness, efficiency or customer satisfaction.

A quality audit is *not* intended to be a:

* verification technique; it cannot replace inspection or testing procedures or activities since it is looking at the QMS not at IT specific services

* method for accepting or rejecting new or amended IT services

* method for supporting an ineffective, inefficient QMS; a quality audit is assessing only a *sample* of activities, at a given point in time, it is unlikely to find all the problems that may exist

* method for assessing the competence of staff; the audit is concerned with the QMS not staff (although a lack of staff training may be identified).

Audit programme
An initial audit programme will have been prepared during Stage 3 of QMS implementation (see 4.1.3). The programme should be reviewed regularly (at least once a year) to ensure that audit effort is being applied effectively.

Audit strategy
An appropriate strategy should be followed for each audit. This will depend upon the audit objectives. For example, an audit could be conducted by following IT service management processes downstream from the receipt of an initial service brief (such as a feasibility study report or a project initiation document) or specification of requirements through the relevant stages of service design, development, testing, installation and delivery. Alternatively, a current service could be selected and followed upstream to see what products were produced relating to it and what records have been kept.

Another approach could be to select a particular IT service management function and follow its involvement in the current services and in services being designed, developed tested and installed.

More details on quality system auditing are given in the QMS Audit volume of the QML.

Documentation of audit results
The organization, policies and procedures for internal audit should have been determined as part of QMS development (4.1.3). In particular, the procedures should ensure that the results of audits are documented and retained as quality records.

The records should identify:

* any non-conformities or deficiencies found

* the corrective action agreed and the responsibility and timescale for its completion.

5.1.4 Customer contract review

ISO 9001 requires that a supplier "shall establish and maintain procedures for contract review...", and that each contract "shall be reviewed by a supplier to ensure that...the requirements are adequately defined and documented...the supplier has the capability to meet contractual requirements..."

For IT Services suppliers, the requirement above applies to:

* proposals or tenders to supply new or modified IT services

* the specification of requirements for new IT services or for modifications to existing services

* SLAs (see the **Service Level Management** module for a definition of an SLA).

It may be that no legal contract exists; for example in the case of a SLA between two parts of the same organization, or between government departments. However, the agreements noted above should be treated as though they were contracts for the purposes of the QMS and the standard (ISO 9001).

The objectives of a contract review are to:

* ensure that the customer's requirements are clearly defined, understood by both IT Services and its customers and recorded

* allow both parties to ensure that they have identified the organization, resources and facilities required to fulfil the contract

* identify, and agree or resolve, any differences between, for example, an invitation to tender and a tender, a tender and a specification of requirements (SoR), an SoR and a service specification and its accompanying service quality control specification and SLA.

Contract review procedures

The procedures for contract review should be defined as part of the QMS, and records of reviews should be made and kept.

5.1.5 Service design

Service design will follow the agreement of a specification of requirements. Service design should be carried out as a PRINCE project or part of one (ISO 9001 requires that service design and development activities be "planned and assigned to qualified personnel equipped with adequate resources"), and should be coordinated with any related application system developments and procurement activities.

Quality plans for new services

The design of a new or modified service should include the preparation of a quality plan. The development of a service quality plan is described in section 4.1.3.2. In order to be able to monitor and control service quality characteristics it may be necessary to build instrumentation into the applications software on which the service will be based. The requirement for such instrumentation should, ideally, be included in the SoR.

Design control

ISO 9001 requires that IT Services "shall establish and maintain procedures to control and verify the design..." of a service in order to ensure that the specified requirements are met. These procedures should include:

* requirements review - to identify and resolve any incomplete, ambiguous or conflicting requirements

* design verification measures such as design reviews and acceptance tests (see the **Testing an IT Service for Operational Use** module for details on operational acceptance testing) to ensure that the design meets the requirements, includes or references acceptance criteria, conforms to any relevant legal or regulatory requirements, includes appropriate quality characteristics and the means to monitor and control or influence them (see quality plans above and in section 4.1.3.2)

* document and change control procedures.

The results of design verification activities should be documented and retained as quality records.

5.1.6 Service quality monitoring and control

In order to improve the quality of its services, IT Services should collect, analyze and act on quantitative measures of service quality.

These measures should be used to:

* take remedial action if metric levels deteriorate, or fall below established target levels

* establish specific service improvement goals.

IT Services should also collect and analyze quantitative measures of the IT service development process to determine:

* how well the development process is being carried out in terms of milestones and in-process quality objectives being met on schedule

* how effective the development process is at reducing the probability that faults are introduced or that any faults go undetected.

In addition, ISO 9001 (ISO 9001 4.10.2) requires that in-process inspection and testing is carried out for all services.

IT Services procedures should include checks on the performance of the relevant quality activities set out in service quality plans. These will include:

* periodic monitoring of processes and service quality characteristics and the reporting of service quality statistics as required by quality plans

* inspection and testing of inputs to the service, processes within the service and outputs from the service

* review of the statistics gathered, and inspection and test results, both against targets for the period and over time.

Where a failure to meet service quality requirements occurs, or is threatened, an investigation into the cause should be carried out. Appropriate action to prevent occurrence or recurrence of the problem should be initiated. This will involve close liaison between the quality management, service level management, problem management and customer liaison functions (and other IT service management functions as appropriate).

Customer satisfaction

As noted in section 5.1.3.1, customer assessments of service quality are an important measure and should form part of service quality monitoring and control. (See the **Customer Liaison** module for more detail on assessing customer satisfaction.)

Section 5
Post-implementation and audit

Management reporting	Detailed, concise reports should be provided regularly to both customers and IT Service managers to show the achievement of quality for each IT service.

5.1.7 Configuration management and change management

Configuration management and change management are core components of the QMS. Configuration management provides a mechanism for identifying, controlling and tracking configuration items. Change management ensures that proposed changes are evaluated, authorized, validated and verified as appropriate, and implemented in a controlled way. Detailed guidance is given in the **Configuration Management**, **Change Management** and **Software Control and Distribution** modules.

5.1.8 Quality improvement

"A continual evaluation of the operation of the service processes should be practised to identify and actively pursue opportunities for service quality improvement." (ISO 9004-2 6.4).

Quality improvement is aimed at identifying better working practices or changes to configuration items which lead to a better IT service for customers or reduced risk and cost for IT Services. Quality improvements must be cost-effective and changes to policy, practice and training should be managed (see 5.1.7) and should only be approved where benefits to customers, the business or personnel will result. Over engineering or refining is not cost-effective.

Process and Programme	Quality improvement should be an on-going process. Proposals for improvements will arise from:

* analysis of incidents (including customer complaints) and problems (see **Help Desk** and **Problem Management**)

* seeking and analysing customer evaluations of the services (see 5.1.3.1)

* IT Services' own assessments of service quality; these should be compared with customer assessments, because IT Services often believes that it is supplying a good service when the customers do not agree (this is often caused by a lack of customer liaison coupled with the use of the wrong measures of service quality, for example, the use of serviceability rather than availability as a measure).

Managers and staff within IT Services should also be encouraged to submit ideas or proposals for improving quality (for example, by the use of suggestion schemes and quality circles, and with recognition for effort and participation).

In addition, management may wish to establish specific quality improvement projects or programmes with the achievement of specific quality objectives in mind.

Communication   It is important that improvements in quality, the progress on quality improvement programmes, successes attributable to the introduction of parts of the quality management system and the timescales for solutions to problems yet to be implemented are periodically reported to all personnel within IT Services. This emphasises management commitment to quality and encourages further improvements. The objective is to make quality improvement a way of life.

More guidance on quality improvement is given in the QMS Implementation volume of the QML.

5.1.9 Training

Initial training requirements will have been established in Stage 3 of the quality initiative (see 4.1.3.4). On-going training is also likely to be required to ensure that IT Services staff are qualified to carry out activities affecting service quality (see 4.1.4.1). ISO 9001 requires that "the supplier shall establish and maintain procedures for identifying the training needs and provide for the training of all personnel performing activities affecting quality".

5.1.10 ISO 9001 certification

Certification to ISO 9001 will demonstrate publicly that IT Services has a commitment to quality, and that:

* the system that it has implemented to manage the quality of its services meets the requirements of an internationally agreed standard

* IT Services follows the policies, procedures and standards of the QMS

* the quality management system is effective in ensuring and maintaining IT service quality.

One of the principal benefits of certification lies in the requirements for surveillance, re-assessment and re-certification. The QMS cannot be allowed to fall into disuse or certification will be withdrawn. This provides an external stimulus to the commitment to the quality management system.

Section 5
Post-implementation and audit

5.2 Dependencies

The policies, procedures and tools to allow for monitoring, reporting and assessing service quality should be in place.

To ensure the ongoing effectiveness of the QMS, it is essential that the top management commitment to service quality improvement, developed prior to and during the QMS implementation initiative, is maintained.

Without this continued commitment the QMS - and IT service quality - is likely to deteriorate over time.

Since internal quality audits are fundamental to the process of identifying both areas of non-conformity within existing procedures and potential areas for improvement it is essential that the audit programme is well designed and that the staff who will conduct internal audits are suitably trained and skilled in the process. The audit process must ensure that audit trail information is formally recorded and available for review to continually measure the effectiveness of the improvement of the QMS via the post-implementation review and regular management reviews.

5.3 People

In a large IT Services organization the Quality Manager will need support. This should be provided by the quality office discussed in section 3.3.

Large IS Directorates or IT Services organizations may wish to appoint a separate internal Quality Audit Manager reporting to the Quality Manager.

The internal Quality Audit Manager or the Quality Manager (if a separate audit manager is not appointed) should prepare a schedule of audits which covers all IT Services functions and all aspects of ISO 9001.

The IS Director or IT Services Manager (depending on the scope of the quality system) should:

* require management reviews of the QMS

* review complaints and the progress of the quality improvement process and programmes.

Management reviews will generally be carried out by, or under the direction of, the Quality Manager.

Quality auditors

Internal audits should be carried out by competent and responsible persons who are not directly involved in the function or procedure being audited so that there is no conflict of interests; this is a key requirement of ISO 9001. Other requirements for quality auditors are set out in section 3.3, and the QMS Audit volume of the QML.

The Service Level Manager should supply the Quality Manager with:

- * reports on service levels achieved against targets
- * assessments of the quality of each service
- * assessments of the progress and results of any customer contract and SLA reviews.

The Customer Liaison Manager should supply assessments of customer satisfaction.

Everyone in IT Services should be involved in quality improvement and the provision of quality IT services. Quality improvement activities and techniques are described in the CCTA Quality Management Library.

5.4 Timing

Quality audit: internal

Internal quality audits should be scheduled on the basis of the status and importance of the activity being audited, and so some may need to be reviewed on a more frequent basis than others.

The internal Quality Audit Manager should prepare a programme of audits at least once a year which sets out the planned timing and frequency of audits. The programme should ensure that each IT Services function, and each requirement of ISO 9001 (possibly on a cross-functional basis - for example, the application of document control or quality record keeping across all IT Services functions) is audited at least once a year.

As the programme progresses, the internal Quality Audit Manager should use the information about the QMS (eg from internal and external audit reports, corrective action and changes to the QMS) to tune the audit programme to give more attention to (for example) functions or parts of the QMS:

- * which are not performing well
- * where a change in the system or organization has occurred
- * which have had fewer audit visits than others.

Section 5
Post-implementation and audit

Quality audit: external	External quality audits are of two main types; second party and third party (see Annex H).
	Second party audits may take place either prior to, or as a result of, an award of contract to IT Services by an external customer (ie a separate legal entity). Second party audits are unlikely to be required if IT Services has an ISO 9001 conformant QMS certified by an accredited assessment organization (see Annex G).
	Third party certification assessments will take place every three years, but more frequent *surveillance visits* by auditors from the certification body will take place at an agreed rate; typically twice a year.
Management review	Management reviews should take place every six to twelve months. It may be useful to schedule reviews so that they are complete before any reviews of SLAs take place.
ISO 9001 certification	Advice on the timing of assessment for certification should be sought from the selected accredited certification body. However, some time - typically six months - should be allowed for the system to "bed down" and for quality records to be produced for the auditors to assess.

The IT Infrastructure Library
Quality Management for IT Services

Section 6
Benefits, costs and possible problems

6. Benefits, costs and possible problems

"An effective quality management system should be designed to satisfy customer needs and expectations while serving to protect the company's interests. A well-structured quality system is a valuable management resource in the optimization and control of quality in relation to risk, cost and benefit considerations"

(ISO 9004 - 1987, 0.4.5).

6.1 Benefits

An effective quality management system will benefit both IT Services and its customers. The principal benefits to IT Services are improved customer satisfaction and net savings in costs. The principal benefits to customers are improved services which meet the business needs and improved service availability.

6.1.1 Benefits to IT Services

> "Quality is free. It's not a gift, but it's free. What costs money are the unquality things – all the actions that involve not doing jobs right the first time.
>
> Quality is not only free, it is an honest-to-everything profit maker. Every penny you don't spend on doing things wrong, over or instead becomes half a penny right on the bottom line ... If you concentrate on making quality certain, you can probably increase your profit by an amount equal to 5 to 10 per cent of your sales. That is a lot of money for free."
>
> *Quality is free: the art of making quality certain –*
> *Philip B Crosby*

Failure to meet service requirements costs money. IT Services benefits from an effective QMS by reducing failure costs (see Annex C.1.4), in particular the costs of service downtime, rework and problem analysis correction. Experience shows that costs due to poor quality can be reduced or even eliminated. The savings in terms of resources and time can be reinvested resulting in higher productivity, and greater efficiency and economy.

In the longer term there is also likely to be a reduction in appraisal costs (in particular in operational acceptance testing costs), and possibly in prevention costs. Other benefits are:

* better targeting of resources for improvements

* improved appraisal and control of suppliers and consultants

* services delivered when required, to specification and to cost.

> **Examples of the benefits to be gained**
>
> Poor planning for a service can lead to insufficient capacity and performance and availability problems, or conversely to increased expenditure. Planning within the context of a QMS, on the other hand, will lead to the selection of an optimum configuration, fewer problems, lower costs and avoid overspend.
>
> Failure to recover from incidents effectively and efficiently leads to prolonged loss of service, and if no systems are in place to investigate the cause of incidents they may repeat with further loss of service and more costs. Installing a QMS will help to ensure that appropriate corrective action is taken in both the short and the longer term.
>
> Services which have been well designed and constructed require less corrective and perfective maintenance and should also cost less to adapt to changing business requirements.

6.1.2 Benefits to customers

The benefits to customers of IT Services from the implementation of a QMS for IT Services arise from having IT services designed, developed, implemented and delivered to meet their functional and non-functional requirements. This gives benefits to customers in two major areas:

* improved service availability; which means more productive time and less cost (eg less enforced idleness, less recovery effort/rework)

* IT services delivered at an agreed level of service and cost (quality service design implies higher user productivity from systems which match the optimal method of working, fewer complaints and so higher IT Services productivity).

Section 6
Benefits, costs and possible problems

Quality services are also more likely to:

* be operational on time, and therefore supply customers with the expected benefits. Late service implementation can cost the customers those anticipated benefits

* deliver higher user productivity over and above the gains from improved availability because they meet the needs of the business and the users (and avoid the need for users to run duplicate manual or PC-based systems)

* allow the users to deliver a better service to their own customers.

In addition, the reduction in IT Services failure costs may lead to reduction in IT Services charges.

6.2 Costs

The costs involved in planning, developing, implementing and running a quality management system and a quality management function are largely staff time and training costs.

The costs of a quality management system and a quality management function can be considered under three headings:

* planning, development and implementation costs

* ongoing running costs

* the costs of quality improvement.

6.2.1 Planning, development and installation costs

The costs of planning, developing and implementing a quality management system will depend on the current standards and practices in an organization. The further that these are from the best practice described in the IT Infrastructure Library and the requirements of ISO 9001, then the higher the costs. The costs comprise:

* the cost of the personnel directly involved in the initiative (in the development of policies and procedures and in internal audits)

* training costs (including the costs of awareness exercises)

* the cost of developing and/or procuring tools

* the cost of modifications to existing applications systems to allow quality criteria to be measured (see service quality plans in section 4.1.3.2

* the costs of any consultants used

* assessment costs (if ISO 9001 certification is sought).

6.2.2 Ongoing running costs

The ongoing running costs of a QMS are principally personnel costs incurred under the prevention and appraisal activities described in section 5, they consist of:

* personnel costs (staffing and managing the quality management function, quality auditing, sub-contractor appraisal)

* training costs for existing and new staff.

They also include the cost of surveillance and re-assessment visits if certification to a quality standard is to be sought and maintained.

6.2.3 The costs of quality improvement

The costs of ongoing quality improvement will be organization-specific. Unless self-evident, each opportunity for quality improvement should be the subject of an investment appraisal.

6.3 Possible problems

Quality management as required by the ISO 9000 series of standards and described in this module is a fairly new subject to most IS Directorates/IT Services organizations, and many lack the skills and experience necessary to carry out the development and management of a QMS.

Lack of management commitment

If, at any time during the development, implementation or maintenance of a QMS senior management lack commitment then staff are also likely to lack commitment and the development, implementation or implemented system will fail. Certification of the QMS by an accredited body, together with its surveillance and re-assessment visits often helps to maintain commitment.

Staff cynicism

Staff may initially be cynical about the quality initiative, and this will lead to a lack of commitment. One of the most important tasks of the project team and management is to

Section 6
Benefits, costs and possible problems

	explain the potential benefits of the QMS from the staff viewpoint and to stress (and demonstrate) management's commitment.
Determination of quality related costs	To provide a detailed and accurate cost/benefit analysis it will be necessary to establish current failure, prevention and appraisal costs, and to estimate the potential benefits. However, it may be difficult, particularly during the feasibility study and development of the quality management system to identify quality related costs with any degree of accuracy or even with any degree of certainty. This may make it difficult to identify and quantify potential benefits and so to justify the development of a QMS.

Examples of quality related costs for IT Services

Prevention costs

Quality planning (including: the planning, development and maintenance of the QMS; the preparation of service quality plans and the instrumentation of application systems; and the design and development of other quality measurement and testing systems), availability, capacity and contingency planning, configuration management, contract review, service design review, operational acceptance testing to demonstrate reliability and maintainability, supplier assurance, quality training, quality auditing, quality improvement programmes, the calibration and maintenance of quality measurement and test systems.

Appraisal costs

Operational acceptance testing to demonstrate conformance to requirements, service level and quality monitoring, inspection and testing of consumables, quality record storage.

Internal failure costs

The costs of staff and idle facilities as a result of service downtime, costs incurred in analyzing incidents and problems to determine causes and remedial actions (ie problem management, the costs of replacement, rework, review and testing of system or service modifications made following service failure or as a result of incident or problem analysis, costs incurred due to the failure of purchased products (eg hardware or software) or services (eg maintenance or testing); these will include the costs of idle facilities and staff.

External failure costs

The investigation of complaints and any compensation, discounts to customers following a failure to meet agreed service levels, loss of customer goodwill (which may eventually lead to the customer obtaining the service elsewhere), cost of product recall (faulty hardware or software items), product liability.

Costs of failing to deliver quality systems are not always readily apparent to senior management. For example, in cases where services are so badly designed and constructed that they are re-developed, then the cost of re-development is a failure cost. However, such costs are often recorded as new service development rather than rework. The feasibility study or project team should endeavour to identify and

	quantify the amount of new development work which is really rework so that the true costs of failure can be established.

Full details on quality costing are given in Chapter 11 of the QMS Implementation volume of the QML. |
Determination of requirements and agreement of realistic SLAs	If service requirements and the functional requirements for the underlying systems are poorly documented and are not up-to-date it may be difficult to agree quality criteria and service levels with users. In particular, it may be difficult to identify and agree realistic - that is required, rather than desired, and achievable service levels.
Raising customer and staff expectations	Unless the purpose, objectives and timescales of the initiative are clearly defined at the start of the initiative customer and staff expectations may be raised too high, and when these unrealistic expectations are not met may lead to the initiative being discredited. The project manager and Customer Liaison Manager should devise a communications strategy for the initiative to ensure that this does not occur.
Failure to obtain certification	Failure to obtain certification at the first attempt may lead to disillusionment amongst staff, and possibly the quality management system being discredited. The build up to certification must be handled carefully; ideally certification should not be sought until IT Services is satisfied that the QMS is complete, conforms to ISO 9001, and is effective. It may be desirable to schedule a "mock" assessment to establish that this is the case.

7. Tools

All the tools described in other IT Infrastructure Library modules are relevant to an effective quality management system. However, those most relevant are:

* a configuration management database to help to identify, track and control changes to IT infrastructure items, including documentation
* testing and validation tools
* incident recording and problem management tools
* availability, capacity and performance measurement tools - to measure service performance against SLAs
* capacity management database to assist with availability, capacity and performance forecasting
* instrumentation in applications software; that is, code which allows some service quality characteristics to be measured
* report generation and statistical analysis tools
* cost management tools - to help to identify the costs of quality
* word processing and graphic presentation software.

The term *tools* includes all inspection, measuring and test equipment. *Equipment* in the context of an IT Services quality management system includes monitoring software, operations (system, installation, acceptance and monitoring) tests, checklists and any software instruments (code to allow some service quality characteristics to be measured) installed in applications systems as well as hardware.

ISO 9001 requires that the supplier "shall control, calibrate and maintain inspection, measuring and test equipment...equipment shall be used in a manner which ensures that measurement uncertainty is known and is consistent with the required measurement capability".

ISO 10012 part 1, *Quality assurance requirements for measuring equipment - Part 1: Metrological confirmation system for measuring equipment* specifies the main features of the confirmation system to be used for a supplier's measuring equipment to help to demonstrate compliance with a specification or SLA.

Tools used for inspection, testing, measuring system performance or software replication should be under configuration management.

The IT Infrastructure Library
Quality Management for IT Services

8. Bibliography

Quality Management Library: CCTA; 1992; ISBN 0 11 330569 9; HMSO.

IT Infrastructure Support Tools (part of the CCTA Appraisal and Evaluation Library): CCTA; 1992; ISBN 0 11 330586 9; HMSO.

Appraisal and Evaluation of IS Strategies (CCTA IS Planning Subject Guides): CCTA; 1991; ISBN 0 946683 425; HMSO.

Strategic Planning for Information Systems (volume A2 of the management and planning set of the CCTA Information System Guides): CCTA; 1989; ISBN 0 471 92522 5; John Wiley and Sons Limited.

TickIT guide to software quality management system construction and certification using EN29001 (issue 2): Department of Trade and Industry; 1992; available from the TickIT Project Office, 68 Newman Street, London W1A 4SE.

Quality is free: the art of making certain; Philip B Crosby; ISBN 0-451-62585-4; New American Library (a paperback reprint of a hardcover edition published by McGraw-Hill Book Company).

For a list of relevant standards see Annex B.

Relevant information will also be found in the following CCTA IS Guides (also published by Wiley - see Strategic Planning for Information Systems above):

A3 Computer and Office Systems Planning

A4 Telecommunications Planning

C1 Services Management

C2 Environmental Services

C3 Contingency Planning

C4 Security and Privacy

C5 Telecommunications Operation and Management.

Annex A. Glossary of terms

Acronyms and abbreviations used in this module

BS	British Standard
CCTA	The Government Centre for Information Systems
CI	Configuration item
CM	Configuration Management
DTI	Department of Trade and Industry
EN	European Norm
FM	Facilities Management
IS	Information System(s)
ISEB	Information Systems Examination Board
ISO	International Standards Organization
IT	Information Technology
NACCB	National Accreditation Council for Certification Bodies
PRINCE	PRojects IN Controlled Environments
QFD	Quality Function Deployment
QML	The CCTA Quality Management Library
QMS	Quality Management System
QSC	Quality Steering Committee
SCT	Service Control Team
SSADM	Structured Systems Analysis and Design Method
SLA	Service Level Agreement
SoR	Statement of Requirements
TED	Technical Environment Description

The IT Infrastructure Library
Quality Management for IT Services

Definitions

	The terminology used in this module is consistent with both ISO 9000-3 and ISO 9004-2.
Availability	The ability of a component or IT service (under combined aspects of its reliability, maintainability and maintenance support) to perform its required function at a stated instant or over a stated period of time. It is usually expressed as the **availability ratio**, ie the proportion of time that the service is actually available for use by the customers within the agreed service time. This is calculated as follows:

$$\frac{\text{(Agreed service time - Downtime)}}{\text{Agreed service time}}$$

Configuration (ISO 2382/IEEE 729)	The requirements, design and implementation that define a particular version of a system or system component.
Configuration Control (ISO 2382/IEEE 729)	The process of evaluating, approving or disapproving, and co-ordinating changes to configuration items after formal establishment of their configuration identification.
Configuration Item (ISO 2382/IEEE 729)	A collection of hardware or software elements treated as a unit for the purpose of configuration management (see also software item).
Configuration Management (ISO 2382/IEEE 729)	The process of identifying and defining the configuration items in a system, controlling the release and change of these items throughout the system life cycle, recording and reporting the status of configuration items and change requests, and verifying the completeness and correctness of configuration items.
Defect (ISO 8402)	The nonfulfilment of intended usage requirements. (Note: The definition covers the departure from or absence of one or more quality characteristics from intended usage requirements. Also see the definition of nonconformity below.)
Downtime	The total period that a service is not operational within an agreed service time (also applicable to IT systems and IT components.
Escalation	Escalation is a process which accesses additional resources, involvement of higher levels of management etc., to ensure that contractual commitments are met.
Failure (ISO 2382/IEEE 729)	The termination of the ability of a hardware element to perform a required function. (Note: hardware can fail but software can only have faults.)

Annex A
Glossary of terms

Fault
(ISO 2382/IEEE 729)

        Hardware: An accidental condition that causes a functional unit to fail to perform its required function.

        Software: A manifestation of an error in software. A fault, if encountered, may cause a failure.

IT service development — All activities to be carried out to create an IT service. IT service development comprises service design and service implementation. Service design and implementation activities are those which transform the purchaser's requirements specification into a service.

IT service quality — The totality of features and characteristics of an IT service that bear on its ability to satisfy stated or implied needs

IT service quality assessment criteria — The set of defined and documented rules and conditions (normally set out in a *quality control specification*) which are used to decide whether the total quality of a specific service is acceptable or not. The quality is represented by the set of rated levels associated with the service.

IT service quality characteristics — A set of attributes of a service by which its quality is described and evaluated. A service quality characteristic may be refined into multiple levels of sub-characteristics.

IT service quality metric — A quantitative scale and method which can be used to determine the value a feature takes for a specific service.

Maintenance (ISO 9000-3) — Maintenance activities for software products may be classified as one of the following:

- **Problem resolution**: which involves the detection, analysis and correction of software nonconformities or defects causing operational problems for users of the software. (When resolving problems, temporary fixes may be used to minimize downtime and permanent modifications carried out later.)

- **Interface modifications**: which may be required when additions or changes are made to the hardware system, or components, controlled by the software

- **Functional expansion or performance improvement**.

Nonconformity (ISO 8402) — The nonfulfilment of specified requirements. (Notes: (1) The definition covers the departure or absence of one or more quality characteristics or quality system elements from specified requirements. (2) The basic difference between "nonconformity" and "defect" (see above) is that specified requirements may differ from the requirements for intended use.)

Operability standard	A standard laid down to help to ensure that application software and other items of the IT infrastructure are produced in a way that makes computer operations more efficient.
Quality control specification	Defines the procedures for evaluating and controlling the *service and service delivery characteristics*; this will form part of the quality plan (it may be a separate document referred to by the plan).
Quality plan (ISO 8402)	The document(s) setting out the specific quality practices, resources and sequence of activities relevant to a particular product, service, contract or project.
Serviceability	The contractual conditions between IT Services and its suppliers covering the availability of, and the conditions under which the contractual conditions are valid for a configuration item or system.
Service delivery specification (ISO 9004-2)	The service delivery specification defines how the required IT service is to be provided.
Service Level Agreement	A written agreement or contract between users and the IT service provider which documents the agreed service levels for an IT service. Typically it will cover: service hours, service availability, user support levels, response times, restrictions and the service levels to be provided in a contingency. It may also include security and accounting procedures.
Service specification (ISO 9004)	A definition of the service to be provided in terms of both functional and non-functional requirements (ie the *what*). Equivalent to an SSADM requirements specification. ISO 9004 requires that the service specification should include: * a description of the *service characteristics* subject to customer evaluation * a standard of acceptability for each service characteristic. See also *specification* and *specified requirements* below.
Software (ISO 9000-3)	Intellectual creation comprising the programs, procedures, rules, and any associated documentation pertaining to the operation of a data processing system. Note: software is independent of the medium on which it is recorded.
Software Item (ISO 9000-3)	Any identifiable part of a software product at an intermediate step or at the final step of development.
Software Product (ISO 9000-3)	Complete set of computer programs, procedures and associated documentation and data designated for delivery to a user.

Annex A
Glossary of terms

Specification (ISO 8402)	The document that prescribes the requirements with which the product or service has to conform.
Specified requirements (BS 5750 part 4)	Either:
	(a) Requirements prescribed by the purchaser and agreed by the supplier in a contract for products and/or services
	(b) Requirements prescribed by the supplier which are perceived as satisfying a market need.
Validation (for software)	The process of evaluating software products to ensure compliance with specified requirements. (Note: the ISO 9000-3 definition has been expanded to include all software products.)
Verification (for software) (ISO 9000-3)	The process of evaluating the (software) products of a given phase to ensure correctness and consistency with respect to the products and standards provided as input to that phase. (Note: in this context, ISO 9000-3 defines phase as a defined segment of work.)

Annex B. Relevant International and British Standards

The guidance in this module is based on ISO 9001. ISO 9001 is part of the ISO 9000 series of standards. The ISO 9000 series of quality standards and guides are an internationally agreed set of quality management and quality assurance standards. They have been developed as a result of the recognition by various countries and industries that certain key aspects of business need to be controlled in order to provide customers with confidence that supplied products and services will satisfy requirements.

The ISO 9000 series of standards is identical to the BS (British Standard) 5750 and EN (European Norm) 29000 series of standards. The ISO 9000 reference numbers are used throughout the module except where there is no ISO equivalent to a British Standard (a table showing the relationship between International Standards (published by the ISO), British Standards (published by the British Standards Institute), and European Standards numbers is given at the end of the Annex).

In addition to the standards described in section 2.5 (ISO-9000, BS 5750 part 4 [ISO 9000-2], ISO 9001, ISO9004 and ISO 9004-2), standards which are particularly relevant to IT Service Management are:

* **ISO 9000 part 3**, *Quality management and quality assurance standards - Part 3: Guidelines for the application of ISO 9001 to the development, supply and maintenance of software*; this guidance document is at the heart of the TickIT project described in Annex D

* **ISO/IEC 9126**, *Information technology - Software product evaluation - Quality characteristics and guidelines for their use*, which defines six characteristics that describe, with minimal overlap, software quality, and describes their use for the evaluation of software quality

* **ISO 10012-1**, *Quality assurance requirements for measuring equipment - Part 1: Metrological confirmation system for measuring equipment*, which specifies the main features of the confirmation system to be used for a supplier's measuring equipment to help to demonstrate compliance with a specification or SLA.

Quality economics

BS 6143, *Guide to the economics of quality*, presents two models for costing quality. Part 2 sets out the *prevention, appraisal and failure* model described in Annex C.1.4). Part 1 sets out a process cost model which describes the modelling

	and determination of the costs of business processes in a manner consistent with total quality management and continuous improvement.
Quality audit	**ISO 10011** is a three part guide to quality systems auditing:

* **ISO 10011 part 1**, *Auditing*, covers basic audit principles, criteria and practices, and provides guidelines for establishing, planning, carrying out and documenting audits of quality systems

* **ISO 10011 part 2**, *Qualification criteria for auditors*, gives guidance on the selection of auditors to perform quality system audits

* **ISO 11011 part 3**, *Managing an audit programme*, gives basic guidelines for managing quality system audit programmes.

Quality vocabulary	ISO 8402 (BS 4778 Part 1), *Quality - Vocabulary*, sets out internationally agreed definitions for quality terms in common use. BS 4778 Part 2 (no ISO equivalent), *Quality concepts and related definitions*, explains concepts and defines terms in quality, management, control, and inspection. BS 4778 Part 3, *Availability reliability and maintainability terms*, presents:

* a glossary of international terms in section 3.2 which includes faults, failures and performance measures; it also provides a vocabulary of quality of service in telecommunications

* a guide to concepts and related definitions in section 3.1 which complements and extends the internationally agreed definitions in section 3.2 by providing conceptual explanations of many of them.

Quality management and quality system elements guidelines	Other relevant parts of **ISO 9004** (*Quality management and quality system elements - guidelines*) currently in draft form are:

* Part 4 - Guidelines for managing quality improvement

* Part 5 - Guidelines for Quality Plans

* Part 6 - Guidelines for Configuration Management.

Software contribution to system reliability	Published in 1992, British Standards Institute Development Draft (DD) 198 provides guidance on assessing the contribution of software to the overall reliability of a system. It outlines procedures for the collection of data for the measurement and prediction of software reliability.

Annex B
Relevant International and British Standards

Total Quality Management	Published in 1992, **BS 7850**, *Total Quality Management*, sets out guidance on the key principles of Total Quality Management (TQM). It emphasises the need for total dedication to the principles of TQM to ensure effective broadcast of the key concepts and attitudes throughout all levels of an organization, and gain the benefits in the areas of customer satisfaction, health and safety, the environment and business objectives.
	BS 7850 concentrates on three key aspects of TQM namely Systems, People and Continuous Improvement. **Part 1 of BS 7850**, *Guide to Management Principles*, is aimed at Senior Management. **Part 2**, *Guide to Quality Improvement Methods*, deals with the implementation of a continuous quality improvement process, and provides a list of the most common tools and techniques available.
Preparation of specifications	**BS 7373**, *Guide to the preparation of specifications*, gives generic guidance on layout, preparation and management.

The IT Infrastructure Library
Quality Management for IT Services

B.1 Relationships between British and International quality standards

Where no entry is shown, no equivalent exists.

British standard	International standard	European standard	Subject
BS 4778 Part 1: 1987	ISO 8402: 1986	EN 28402: 1991	Quality vocabulary - International terms
BS 4778 Part 2: 1991			Quality concepts and related definitions
BS 4778 Part 3, section 3.1: 1991	IEC 50(191): 1990 (related but not equivalent standard)		Availability, reliability and maintainability terms - Part 3 section 3.1: Guide to concepts and related definitions
BS 4778 Part 3, section 3.2: 1991	IEC 50(191): 1990		Availability, reliability and maintainability terms - Part 3 section 3.2: Glossary of international terms.
BS 5750 Part 0, section 0.1: 1987	ISO 9000: 1987	EN 29000: 1987	Quality management and quality assurance standards - Guidelines for selection and use
BS 5750 Part 0, section 0.2: 1987	ISO 9004: 1987	EN 29004: 1987	Quality management and quality system elements - Guidelines
BS 5750 Part 1: 1987	ISO 9001: 1987	EN 29001: 1987	Quality systems - Model for quality assurance in design/development, production installation and servicing
BS 5750 Part 2: 1987	ISO 9002: 1987	EN 29002: 1987	Quality systems - Model for quality assurance in production and installation
BS 5750 Part 3: 1987	ISO 9003: 1987	EN 29003: 1987	Quality systems - Model for quality assurance in final inspection and test
BS 5750 Part 4: 1990	ISO 9000-2 (not yet published)		Guide to the use of BS 5750 Part 1, Part 2 and Part 3/ISO 9001, 9002, 9003

Annex B
Relevant International and British Standards

British standard	International standard	European standard	Subject
BS 5750 Part 8: 1991	ISO 9004-2: 1991		Quality systems - Guide to quality management and quality systems elements for services
BS 5750 Part 13: 1991	ISO 9000-3: 1991		Guidelines for the application of BS 5750 Part 1/ISO 9001/EN 29001 to the development, supply and maintenance of software
	ISO/IEC 9126: 1991		Information technology - Software product evaluation - Quality characteristics and guidelines for their use
BS 6143 Part 1: 1992			Guide to the economics of quality - Part 1: Process cost model
BS 6143 Part 2: 1990			Guide to the economics of quality - Part 2: Prevention, appraisal and failure model
BS 7229 Part 1: 1991	ISO 10011-1: 1990		Quality system auditing
BS 7229 Part 2: 1991	ISO 10011-2: 1991		Qualification criteria for quality system auditors
BS 7229 Part 3: 1991	ISO 10011-3: 1991		Managing an quality system audit programme
	ISO 10012-1: 1992		Quality assurance requirements for measuring equipment - Part 1: Metrological confirmation system for measuring equipment
BS 7373: 1991			Guide to the preparation of specifications
BS 7850 Part 1: 1992			Total quality management - Guide to management principles
BS 7850 Part 2: 1992			Total quality management - Guide to quality improvement methods

Annex C. Quality and IT service concepts

This annex describes some of the fundamental concepts relating to a quality management system for IT Services. Important quality concepts are introduced in section C.1, and relevant IT service concepts are described in section C.2. (Relevant quality initiatives are described in Annex D.)

C.1 Quality concepts

C.1.1 IT service quality

There are many definitions of *quality*, such as "fitness for use", "fitness for purpose", "customer satisfaction" or "conformance to requirements". Each of these definitions represents only certain facets of quality, and fuller explanations are usually required which lead to the internationally agreed definition of quality used in this module: "the totality of features and characteristics of a product or service that bear on its ability to satisfy stated or implied needs" (ISO 8402 - 1986).

A *quality* service, therefore, is one which is fit for its purpose and which satisfies customer requirements *both stated and implied*.

Stated needs
: Stated needs are those set out in the customer's specification of requirements. For an IT service they should include a complete, consistent and unambiguous set of functional and non-functional requirements necessary to satisfy the customer's need. Non-functional requirements may include, but are not limited to, availability, reliability, usability, efficiency, maintainability, portability, contingency, levels of support and constraints.

Service requirements need to be clearly defined in terms of characteristics that are observable and subject to customer evaluation. These will form the basis of an SLA (see **Service Level Management**).

The specification of requirements for an IT service may consist of more than one document: for example, the required systems specification, selected technical option specification and design objectives specification for an application system specified using SSADM.

Implied needs
: Where an IT service is being developed as the result of a contract or internal agreement then all needs should - in theory - be specified, and ISO 9001 makes it the supplier's responsibility to ensure that the requirements are adequately defined and documented. However, particularly

in information systems/services development, it is likely that there will be implied needs not addressed in the specification.

In this context, implied needs will be those requirements that are so basic or "obvious" that nobody thinks of them or thinks that they need to be included in the specification, or will be requirements which lie in areas outside the competence of those developing the specification (which often relate to the delivery of the IT service). They will be determined by the nature of the product or service, the customer's organization or the environment within which it operates. It is often a failure to satisfy implied needs which leads to complaints about "poor quality".

To help to overcome the problem of incomplete specification of requirements, IT Services Management should, wherever possible, be involved during the analysis and specification of requirements and during any tendering exercise (see **Software Lifecycle Support**).

Grade

The quality of a product or service should not be confused with its grade. Grade is an indicator of category or rank related to features or characteristics that cover different sets of needs for products or services intended for the same functional use. For example: in an aircraft operated by a company which provides a quality service, a first class aircraft seat is of a higher grade than a standard class seat in that it is luxurious whilst doing what is required of it (transporting a customer from A to B).

Quality must be "built in"

Quality is part of the fabric of an IT service (by definition quality is a function of "the totality of features and characteristics"). While some aspects of service quality can be improved after implementation (additional hardware can be added to improve performance for example), others - particularly aspects such as the reliability and maintainability of applications software - rely on quality being "built in", since to attempt to add it at a later stage is in effect redesign and redevelopment; normally at a much higher cost than if it had been done during the original development. Even in the hardware example quoted above it is likely to cost more to add capacity after service implementation rather than as part of the original project.

A quality approach to developing IT services seeks to get it "right first time", by ensuring that first the design and then the developed and procured components of the service meet the requirements without wastage and reworking.

Annex C
Quality and IT service concepts

C.1.2 Quality Management

Quality management is a systematic way of ensuring that all the activities necessary to design, implement, deliver and improve IT services take place as planned.

There are three major aspects of this: what should IT Services be doing, how should they do it, and how can what is being done be improved. (This third aspect helps to address the problem of implied needs, as customers' views of services are reviewed, areas of complaint or disappointment will often relate to implied needs.)

Organizations which intend to develop and implement quality management tend to do so for one of two reasons:

* either a desire to ensure that the products and services offered meet customer requirements and do things right first time
* or "because it is required" or "for marketing reasons".

In order to implement quality management ISO 9000 recommends that organizations should develop a quality philosophy, a quality policy, quality objectives and a quality management system. Those whose philosophy is based on a determination to improve the service offered in order to satisfy customer's requirements and to do things right the first time will generally succeed. Those who implement a quality system because it is imposed upon them or solely to improve their marketing position will generally fail.

Quality philosophy, quality objectives and other aspects of a quality management system are discussed in section 3.1.

C.1.3 Quality Management System (QMS)

A quality management system (QMS) is a vehicle for delivering quality management. It embraces "the organizational structure, responsibilities, procedures, processes and resources for implementing quality management" (ISO 8402 - 1986).

A QMS has two interrelated aspects: the supplier's needs and interests, and the customer's needs and expectations. The supplier needs to reach and maintain the desired and agreed quality at an optimum cost. The customer needs to have confidence in the ability of the supplier to deliver and maintain that quality.

Each of these aspects requires that objective evidence is recorded and analyzed to demonstrate that the required quality is being planned for and met.

The need for quality to be built in implies that, ideally, a QMS should cover application system specification and development, service management and application system maintenance (ie the full service lifecycle). Where possible, IT Services should be involved in specification and development to ensure that the requirements being specified are realistic and achievable (and therefore that the customers will be satisfied), to enable them to plan for the design and introduction of the new service, and to ensure that any applications software being developed will meet operational requirements. (See Annex C and **Software Lifecycle Support** for more detail on the relationships between development, service management and maintenance.)

C.1.4 Cost of quality

In the past IT Services organizations have often reported on the quality of the services provided only in terms of availability/serviceability, and the number of incidents and the mean time to repair. While these are essential metrics, the true effect of quality or the lack of it should be reported in financial terms since service failures, however caused, cost money, as do preventative quality control activities and quality appraisal activities . Organizations are usually prepared to allocate additional resources to quality related activities if sufficient benefit can be shown.

Classification of quality related costs

Quality related costs can be classified as:

* prevention costs - the costs of planning, systems/ procedures and training for the investigation, prevention or reduction of failures; they include the implementation, operation, maintenance and improvement of a quality management system

* appraisal costs - the costs of measuring the level of achievement of the organization's quality objectives; they include the costs of inspection, testing and measurement

* internal failure costs - the costs associated with failures to achieve specified requirements which are detected before ownership of the product or service is transferred to the customer; they include the costs of defect analysis, reworking and wasted resources

Annex C
Quality and IT service concepts

* external failure costs - the costs associated with failure to achieve specified requirements after ownership of the product or service has been transferred to the customer; they include the costs of recalling, reworking and reissuing products, and of dealing with customer complaints and enquiries; they also include the value of some losses which are not readily represented in financial terms, for example, loss of customer goodwill and loyalty, reduction in market share and loss of reputation.

Quality related costs as defined in BS 6143 Part 2, *Guide to the economics of quality - Part 2: Prevention, appraisal and failure model* do not include the costs of poor quality IT services for customers. The costs of poor quality IT services for customers should always be borne in mind. The loss of goodwill and loyalty referred to above may be the result of real and significant financial loss. For example, customers may be unable to accept orders, record payments etc. If IT Services customers are part of the same organization, then potential savings to customers should be taken into account in the business case for a QMS.

Investment in prevention can substantially reduce internal and external failure costs. This is shown in figure C1.

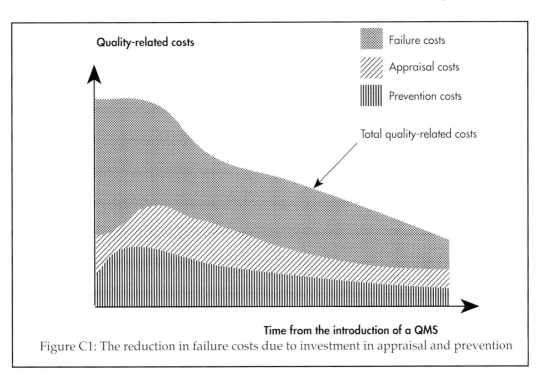

Figure C1: The reduction in failure costs due to investment in appraisal and prevention

An increased awareness of the cost to the organization of quality failure leads:

* first to an increase in the appraisal of service quality

* then to an increase in spending on prevention as appraisal and investigation identify areas where improvements can be made

* finally to a reduction in quality related costs as improvements and preventive action take effect and prevention, appraisal and failure costs reduce.

See section 6 for more detail on the benefits, costs and possible problems of a quality management system.

C.1.5 Total Quality Management

Installing a quality management system is the first step in a process of continuous quality improvement. Section 5 Post-implementation and audit, and BS 7850, *Total Quality Management* give guidance on the implementation of a continuous quality improvement process.

C.2 IT service concepts

This section of the annex describes some IT service concepts for those familiar only with quality.

The IT Service concepts discussed are:

* The components of an IT service (C.2.1)

* Strategic and tactical planning for IT services (C.2.2)

* The IT service lifecycle (C.2.3)

* The scope of a QMS for IT Services (C.2.4).

C.2.1 The components of an IT service

A service is defined as: "the results generated, by activities at the interface between supplier and the customer and by supplier internal activities, to meet customer needs". (ISO-9004-2, 3.5).

An IT service is a service whose results are generated principally by using information technology (IT). An IT service will generally be provided by a combination of computer hardware, systems software, application software (which may be bespoke or packaged), communications equipment and software, trained service delivery and support staff working to appropriate (documented) policies and procedures, and consumable items such as disks, tapes and paper. All these aspects of the service should be designed.

C.2.2 Strategic and tactical planning for IT services

The need for an IT service is driven by business needs. These can change significantly and rapidly due to market forces, economic climate and competition as well as Ministerial decisions, changes in legislation, and internal policy decisions. IT service providers must maintain an awareness of these factors in order to be able to respond to changing business needs with quality services in a timely and cost effective manner. Linking IT service planning and provision to business planning via strategic and tactical information systems planning is essential to achieve this.

The **Planning and Control for IT Services** module of the IT Infrastructure Library gives guidance on how this should be achieved. (See also CCTA IS Guide A2 for information on strategic information systems planning.)

C.2.3 The IT service lifecycle

An IT service is usually conceived, born and implemented in response to a business need, and generally will eventually die when the need changes and the service can no longer be modified to meet it. This sequence of conception, birth, life and eventual death is often described as the IT service *lifecycle*.

Many models of service lifecycles exist, one such model - based on the PRINCE and SSADM methodologies used in Central Government - showing how the various components of a service are identified, specified, developed and managed - is described below. The key point is that IT service managers should be involved as early as possible in the definition of requirements for an IT service, and that wherever possible application software developers and IT service managers should cooperate on the development of an IT service.

(This subject is addressed in more detail in the **Software Lifecycle Support** module, which also describes various lifecycle models).

COMPARISON OF ISO, PRINCE & SSADM PHASES		
ISO model	PRINCE methodology	SSADM methodology
Feasibility study or market research & analysis	**Feasibility study**	**Feasibility study**
Requirements specification	Initiation stage	Requirements analysis Stage 1: Investigation of current environment
	Requirements specification stage	Stage 2: Business system options
		Requirements specification Stage 3: Definition of requirements
Service development Design	Logical system specification stage	Logical system specification Stage 4: Technical system options / Stage 5: Logical design
	Physical design stage	**Physical design**
	Construction stage	
	Operational testing stage	
Installation		Not applicable
	Installation stage	
Service delivery / Servicing	Not applicable	

Shading shows alternate phases within each model. Although the ISO model shows development as a single phase, both ISO 9000-3 and ISO 9004-2 recognise the need to divide development into a number of phases for control. The PRINCE model shown is an example only.

Annex C
Quality and IT service concepts

The PRINCE/SSADM lifecycle	A model based on PRINCE and SSADM splits the IT service lifecycle into several stages. For example:

* feasibility study
* requirements analysis
* requirements specification
* logical system specification
* physical design of applications software, and service delivery
* applications software construction and testing, software and hardware procurement, development of service delivery and quality control specifications
* installation
* service delivery and maintenance
* decommissioning.

The objectives and products of each of these stages are described briefly below, together with a discussion on the possible/desirable involvement of IT Service staff at each stage.

Strictly speaking, ISO 9001 does not cover requirements specification, but only service design onwards. Service design activities start with SSADM stages 4 and 5 (technical system options and logical design). However, ISO 9004 states that the quality system typically applies to, and interacts with, "all activities pertinent to the quality of a product or service. It involves all phases from the initial identification to final satisfaction of requirements and customer expectations".

A quality system for IT service delivery should ideally cover not only service delivery and support activities, but also service specification (including analysis of requirements) and maintenance activities; ie the QMS should cover application software analysis, specification, design and maintenance, as well as the specification of other service delivery procedures. That is, ideally, the QMS should be planned and implemented on an IS Directorate-wide basis.

IT service feasibility study	A feasibility study will define an initial set of requirements for a new or modified IT service, define various business and technical options to satisfy the requirements, assess the organizational impact of each option and consider the business and technical feasibility of the proposed IT service.

Ideally, the feasibility study will be undertaken in the context of a information systems strategy which will have identified the most likely technical environment for a given service. However, even if this is the case (for example, new business opportunities may have been identified, or problems may have arisen in part of the business) the study should consider a number of business and technical options for service provision.

IT Services can and should be involved in the feasibility study from the start, and should aim to supply capacity and cost estimates based on in-house provision of the various technical options identified (clearly the feasibility study team may also wish to consider external provision).

Where a feasibility study is considering the replacement or modification of an existing service or services then IT Services should supply a description of the current service, analyses of service levels (including comparisons of customer and supplier evaluations of service provision), service quality (including outstanding problems and the corrective action to be taken) and information on current or planned quality initiatives which relate to the service(s) under consideration.

The results of the feasibility study will give an early indication of new service requirements and the timescales for their provision. These should be fed into IT Services capacity and (if appropriate) procurement planning.

Requirements analysis	Several types of IT Services input are useful during the requirements analysis stage. In general this will be similar information to that provided during the feasibility study, but during requirements analysis will probably be provided in more detail. The information to be provided will include information on the quality, cost, performance, resource utilisation and reliability of any relevant existing services from the service level management, problem management, customer liaison, cost management, performance management, capacity management and availability management functions.
Requirements specification	During requirements specification IT Services must ensure that operability requirements and operational acceptance criteria are included in the specification and should be involved in confirming that the non-functional requirements have been identified and specified in such a way as to enable the service quality characteristics to be determined.

Annex C
Quality and IT service concepts

	For bespoke software the requirements should include the development of programs or code to enable service quality to be measured. Several of the requirements and other products such as the user role/function matrix will be input to the draft SLA(s).
Logical system specification	Logical system specification is the start of the IT service design process; in particular, the definition and selection of technical options will require capacity and cost information from IT Services. To complete technical environment descriptions (TEDs) will require input on configuration and sizing, training requirements, impact analysis, operational testing, procurement strategy (if relevant) and implementation. The selected TED will be a major input to the design of the service delivery process.
	The products of the logical design activities will input to development of help desk and operations procedures for the service.
Physical design	The physical design of applications software may require data management, availability management, performance management and network management input. The service delivery procedures should be designed in parallel with the applications software, and in particular, the service quality plan prepared.
Applications software	Whilst applications software construction and testing is taking place the service delivery specification (see section 4.1.3.1) should be prepared. Operational acceptance testing (see **Testing an IT Service for Operational Use**) should cover the procedures, hardware and software and the interfaces between them.
Installation	Configuration Management, Help Desk, Problem Management and Customer Liaison are essential functions during the installation process. The installation process is described in **Computer Installation and Acceptance** and **Software Control and Distribution**.
Service delivery and maintenance	Service delivery and maintenance are the subject of the Service Delivery, Service Support, Computer Operations and Networks sets of the IT Infrastructure Library and are not discussed further here.

C.2.4 The scope of a QMS for IT Services

A QMS for IT Services may developed as part of an organization-wide initiative, as part of an IS Directorate-wide initiative or for IT Services alone. The first of these is the preferred option; the third the least desirable, but possibly the most likely, particularly if IT Services are being considered for market testing.

In discussing the scope of an ISO 9000 conformant QMS for IT Services three concepts are particularly important: "purchaser", "supplier" and "sub-contractor".

Purchaser
: The "purchaser" in ISO 9000 terms is the customer; that is, the organization or person who requires the product or the service to be performed.

Supplier
: The "supplier" is the organisation or person supplying the product or performing the service, in this case IT Services.

Sub-contractor
: A "sub-contractor" supplies products or services to the "supplier" which form part of the required product or service, or which are used to produce or deliver the required product or service. These are generally referred to as suppliers in the IT Infrastructure Library.

Applications development and IT Services as a single supplier
: Perhaps the most common model for the supply of IT services is by an organization (either internal or external) where the applications development organization and IT services organization are regarded as a single supplier. That is, the Purchaser - the part or parts of the parent organization requiring the products and service - places a purchase order on the IS Directorate to develop one or more application systems and to provide the IT service based on them. Generally in this case, the Supplier (in the form of the Applications Development and IT Services Divisions of the IS Directorate) will also help the purchaser to specify the requirements for the applications systems and the IT service.

The IS Directorate may "sub-contract" all or part of the systems specification, development and implementation to an external contractor or contractors - sub-contractors in the context of the original purchase.

In order to implement the service it may be necessary to procure additional hardware and systems software and these "products" will be supplied by sub-contractors (external suppliers) to the IS Directorate.

Annex C
Quality and IT service concepts

Once the IT service is implemented IT Services is likely to sub-contract hardware and systems software maintenance. Applications software maintenance may be carried out either by Applications Development, a unit within IT Services, or a sub-contractor.

In this case, the QMS should be designed to cover the IS Directorate as a whole - and the whole of the service lifecycle - not just Applications Development or Service Management - with ISO 9000-3 forming the basis of those parts of the QMS implemented for Applications Development, and the guidance in this module as the basis for those parts of the QMS implemented for IT Services.

Applications development and IT Services as separate suppliers

The next model to consider is the case where applications are developed by one supplier (either internal or external) and the IT service provided by another (again, either internal or external).

In this case, both the applications developer and the service provider are suppliers to the purchaser, and each will have their own quality management system.

From the viewpoint of the service provider, the applications software will be purchaser supplied product (if either the applications software is purchased by the purchaser and then passed to the service provider for incorporation in the IT service or if the applications developer sub-contracts the service provider to run the IT service), or purchased product (if the purchase has been made through the service provider with the applications developer as a sub-contractor).

In any event, the IT service provider will be responsible for preparing the service delivery specification and service quality plan in response to the requirements specification, for agreeing a SLA and, if appropriate, sub-contracting the maintenance of service components. Even in this situation, it is desirable for IT Services to be involved in developing the requirements specification if possible.

Annex D. Relevant quality initiatives

This annex describes quality initiatives relevant to IT service management.

D.1 The Citizen's Charter

In July 1991 the Government presented the "Citizen's Charter" (Cm 1599) to Parliament. The charter is intended to be the most comprehensive programme ever to raise quality, increase choice, secure better value and extend accountability. It is essentially a statement of ideas and initiatives to stimulate ways in which standards of service provision by public service bodies may be raised using methods appropriate to each service provider.

The four main themes of the Charter concern Quality, Choice, Standards and Value, all of which may be significantly improved for the customer by the implementation of a formal, structured approach to the provision of product and service quality.

As the Charter states:

"This involves deciding what quality to aim for, the quality that is most cost-effective and appropriate; and then organizing systems to ensure that it is delivered and maintained. Some public service (sector) bodies and parts of government departments (for example the Information Technology Services Agency in the Department of Social Security, and the Import Licensing Branch of the DTI) are using British Standards for Quality Management (BS 5750) to improve the quality of their work. We expect many more to follow."

D.2 Competing for quality

The ideas contained within the Citizen's Charter have been taken further within the "Competing for Quality" White Paper (Cm 1730) which was presented to Parliament during November 1991. In essence the White Paper sets out proposals for the expansion of competition within the public sector and emphasizes the role of public sector managers in buying public and private services on behalf of the public themselves and obtaining value for money.

A key element in the process of obtaining and providing value for money is market testing. The White Paper stresses that this often lengthy process will be streamlined both in consideration of existing services provided by government departments and also for new services, so that cost benefits can be delivered without undue delay. This will be achieved by encouraging competitive tendering for services as early as possible. In the case of entirely new services the government's view is that they should be contracted out, subject of course to requirements and relative value for money.

In keeping with this new approach to market testing the White Paper states that new areas of competition will be opened up within departments nearer to the heart of the government. In particular, "the delivery of clerical and executive operations, specialist and professional skills, and a wide range of facilities management approaches."

These new areas will require market testing to discover the extent to which the private sector can offer new ideas, skills and experience.

In order to ensure that IT services are ready for a market testing exercise it is desirable that certain key elements of a Quality Management System are in place covering such aspects as Service Level Agreements, Quality Planning and Training. In particular, without formally agreed Service Level Agreements in place competitive tendering would prove to be difficult as would the monitoring of achieved service levels in any subsequent contract.

It is therefore recommended that IT Services should consider the following areas of a Quality Management System prior to a market testing exercise:

* the provision of adequate, trained personnel
* definition of Service Level Agreements
* communication and interface links with customers
* service quality measurement procedures.

D.3 The TickIT Project

The publication of the ISO series of quality standards in 1987, served as the trigger for the TickIT Project set up by the Department of Trade and Industry (DTI) to look at the application of such standards to the developed software and to the IS and IT industries. The DTI commissioned studies in this respect and found that the cost of poor quality software within the UK was significant, and that the industry did indeed desire a certification scheme for software.

A follow-up study was conducted by the British Computer Society and produced some draft guidance material for an acceptable certification scheme. The onward development of this draft material has become known as the TickIT Project which has the expressed aim of achieving consistently high standards in software development through the TickIT Quality System Certification Scheme.

The guidance information is produced in the form of the TickIT Guide which contains ISO 9000 part 3 - "Guidelines for the application of ISO 9001 to the development, supply and maintenance of software" (identical to BS 5750 part 13), and specific guidance to both purchasers and suppliers of software for the interpretation of ISO 9001 and guidance for auditors of TickIT certified quality systems.

Where possible purchasers of software (including IT Services departments) should require suppliers to be TickIT certified.

The DISC (Delivering IT Solutions to Customers) Committee which was formerly the IT Assessment Guides Committee is now a focal point for the further development of the TickIT Scheme. Sponsored by the DTI, it will address the scheme's evolution and take account of changing needs of IT Users, European developments and other comments from the IT industry worldwide.

D.4 Vision 2000

The publication of the ISO 9000 series of quality standards and guidelines in 1987 together with the accompanying terminology standard ISO 8402 - 1986, Quality - Vocabulary, has brought harmonisation on a worldwide scale and has supported the growing impact of quality as a factor in international trade.

As a result on ongoing discussion of the ISO 9000 series by ISO technical committee TC176, "Vision 2000" recommendations have been made regarding the further development of the ISO 9000 standards. The basis for Vision 2000 is the recognition of the direction in which current market trends are going, and the fact that there is a migration towards products that are combinations of two or more generic product categories such as hardware, software and services. For instance many products today include the production of computer software, hardware and firmware within which the provision of service aspects such as support and maintenance are essential features.

Consequently Vision 2000 is concerned with the development of a single quality management standard (an updated ISO 9004 that includes new topics as appropriate) together with an updated ISO 9001 and a road-map standard in the form of an updated ISO 9000. The target date for implementing Vision 2000 is 1996.

Annex E. Applying ISO 9001 to IT Services

ISO 9001 provides a generic model for quality assurance in design/development, production, installation and servicing. This annex provides an overview of how to apply ISO 9001 to IT Services, and should be read in conjunction with ISO 9001. Where relevant, it refers to other IT Infrastructure Library modules which provide more detail. You should also read the CCTA Quality Management Library (QML) and ISO 9004 part 2: "Quality management and quality system elements - Part 2: Guidelines for services".

For relevant definitions, please refer to the glossary in Annex A.

This annex follows the structure of ISO 9001 Section 4: Quality system requirements. ISO 9001 headings are used and paragraph numbers are given in square brackets after the section heading, for example: Management responsibility [4.1] - where 4.1 is the ISO 9001 reference.

E.1 Management responsibility [4.1]

E.1.1 Quality policy [4.1.1]

To comply with the requirements of ISO 9001, and for the quality management system (QMS) to succeed, IT Services management must define, document, and maintain a quality philosophy, policies and objectives. They must then ensure that the IT Services quality philosophy, policies, objectives and the supporting quality management system are understood, implemented and maintained at all levels of the organization.

Ideally, the QMS for IT Services will be part of a larger organization-wide system - see section 3.1.4, Annex C.2.4, and the **Software Lifecycle Support** module of the IT Infrastructure Library - and the philosophy and policies will be one part of the management policies developed within an IS strategy study (see the CCTA Information Systems Guide A2 and the **Planning and Control for IT Services** module). An IT Services-specific quality policy may stand alone, but ideally should exist as part of the IS quality policy.

An example of an IT Services quality philosophy and goals is given in section 3.1.7 of this module. The QMS Implementation volume of the QML also contains guidance on establishing a quality philosophy and policies. ISO 9004-2 (5.2.2 and 5.2.3) contains guidance on quality policy, goals and objectives for service organizations.

All personnel involved in any part of the specification of requirements, service design/development, installation, service delivery, service support or maintenance of IT services should be required to adhere to the policies and procedures set out in the IT Services quality management system documentation (see section E.2).

E.1.2 Organization [4.1.2]

E.1.2.1 Responsibility and authority [4.1.2.1]

All IT Services managers, in conjunction with the Quality Manager, are responsible for ensuring that all employees are trained so that they understand the business and quality management system policies and objectives, and the commitment required to achieve these objectives.

The IS Director, IT Services Manager, Service Level Manager and Customer Liaison Manager are responsible for ensuring, as appropriate, that customers are aware of IT Services quality philosophy.

Before a new service is developed IT Services Management is responsible for ensuring that all the necessary resources, are available.

Management are also responsible for ensuring that all those involved in service design are aware of their responsibilities for achieving service quality. ISO 9004-2(6.2.2) provides more detail on design responsibilities.

IT Services' customers also have a management responsibility to help to ensure a quality service. In particular, customers should cooperate with IT Services to provide all the information necessary to design or monitor a service when it is required. Customers should also assign a representative with the authority to deal with contractual matters and ensure that the customer observes agreements made with IT Services (see **Service Level Management**).

Each person in IT Services should be responsible for ensuring his or her work meets the required standards of quality. Positions which have responsibility for key elements of the quality management system and processes and the formal reporting lines between them should be shown on an organization structure chart. Key elements include: control and maintenance of the QMS; control of the corrective action system; control to ensure that corrective actions taken are effective; management reviews of the QMS.

Annex E
Applying ISO 9001 to IT Services

The responsibilities and authority of *all* personnel who manage, perform and verify work affecting quality need to be defined together with any interrelationships. Ideally, job descriptions should be prepared. While each job description should state identified requirements for liaison with other positions, management should encourage personnel to discuss quality related issues with others if they believe that it is necessary or desirable in order to maintain or improve the quality of IT services. Job descriptions should also include any document control responsibilities. See **IT Services Organization** for job descriptions for IT service management roles.

The definitions given in the QMS Implementation volume of the QML will help in documenting the responsibilities of those staff who manage, perform or verify work affecting quality.

In assigning responsibilities for service design, management should ensure that all staff are aware of their responsibility for achieving service quality. These responsibilities include:

* planning, preparation, validation, maintenance and control of service specifications

* specifying products and services to be procured for the service delivery process

* implementing design reviews for each phase of the service design

* validating that the service delivery process, as implemented, meets the service requirements.

Organization and responsibilities are also covered by the **Customer Liaison**, **Testing Software for Operational Use** and **Computer Installation and Acceptance** modules. Reference should also be made to the **Managing Facilities Management** module section 2.3.

Developing and delivering a quality service to the customer requires cooperation between the IT service provider (the supplier) and the customer. The customer should therefore assign a representative to deal with the IT services supplier on all matters, but the following in particular:

* defining the customer's requirements

* answering the IT services supplier's questions

* approving the IT services supplier's proposals

* concluding agreements with the IT services supplier

* taking responsibility for supplying any products or services to the IT services supplier, which may form part of the service agreement.

E.1.2.2 Verification resources and personnel [4.1.2.2]

IT Services must recognise the importance of verification and validation activities in assuring the quality of its services. In-house verification and validation requirements should be identified and recorded in appropriate procedures manuals. Verification and validation responsibilities should be defined in the job descriptions mentioned in E.1.2.1 above.

ISO 9001 requires that staff responsible for the verification or validation activities need to be qualified by education, training or experience. This requirement must be taken into account when planning for a new or revised IT Services organization, new or amended service, or IT infrastructure development/change projects.

It should be noted that verification requirements apply to hardware, systems software and tools as well as application software; so IT Services (the supplier in ISO 9001 terms) must have, or have access to, the relevant expertise.

Guidance on the responsibility for such verification is given in the **Testing an IT Service for Operational Use** and **Computer Installation and Acceptance** modules.

It is important that design reviews and audits are carried out by personnel independent of those responsible for performing the work. This applies to all the reviews and audits described in Section 5 of each IT Infrastructure Library module. A small organization may find this requirement difficult to satisfy, and consequently it may be necessary to seek external assistance.

Service quality should be assessed by the IT services supplier; by, for example, verifying service deliverables against the customer's requirements. In addition the IT services supplier should assess quality as perceived by the customer. Both these approaches are covered in Section 5 of the **Service Level Management** module.

Note that **Testing an IT Service for Operational Use** recommends that operational testing (which includes system, installation and acceptance) is carried out independently of development and maintenance and that it gives suggestions on how the function should be organized (section 3.3.1). These recommendations will have a significant impact on development contracts let to external organizations with ISO 9001 TickIT certification since ISO 9000-3 [5.7.4] requires the developer to validate its operation as a complete product before offering the product for delivery and purchaser acceptance (a solution may be to contract a team under the management of the in-house test manager from the developer). In-house development projects are more straightforward provided that the IS organization as a whole is regarded as the supplier.

E.1.2.3 Management representative [4.1.2.3]

A management representative needs to be nominated who will be responsible for all matters affecting the QMS. Responsibilities and authority must be defined and the representative's position in the organization shown on an organization structure chart.

Clearly, the IS Director and IT Services Manager are responsible for ensuring that IT Services provides quality services. However, the authority and responsibility for ensuring that the requirements of ISO 9001 are met (and in particular, that IT Services quality policy, quality management system and related procedures are understood, implemented and maintained at all levels in the organization) may be delegated (to the Quality Manager for example).

Although the representative acts as a focal point for quality matters, it is important to remember that the whole workforce contributes to the overall quality of products and services.

The management representative need not necessarily be a member of the IS Directorate or IT Services. If not, then the IS or IT Quality Manager will need to work closely with the management representative.

This is addressed in section 3.1.6 and the **IT Services Organization** module.

E.1.3 Management review [4.1.3]

The IT Services management team should periodically review the quality management system to ensure that:

* the quality management system meets the requirements of ISO 9001

* the organization has been and is continuing to adhere to the requirements of the quality management system; or that effective corrective action has been taken if the requirements have not been met

* the quality management system is effective in ensuring that the quality of IT services meets the specified or contractual requirements and in improving the quality of products and services.

Management reviews will normally be carried out once or twice a year. Additional management reviews may be carried out if the management team considers it to be necessary or desirable.

Management reviews should include:

* results of service performance analysis: how effective and efficient was the service delivery in meeting the service requirement and achieving customer satisfaction?

* results of internal audits of the effectiveness of the quality system in achieving the objectives of service quality

* changes brought about by advances in technology, quality concepts, market strategies etc.

Records of management reviews are quality records and need to be retained (see E.16).

For further guidance, reference should be made to section 5 of this and all other IT Infrastructure Library modules.

E.2 Quality system [4.2]

The quality management system brings together all the functions, objectives and activities which contribute to the quality of the IT services being provided. It needs to be documented and this will normally take the form of a Quality Manual (see section 4.1.3.1), and related standards, methodologies and work instructions.

Each of these documents must be subject to the defined document control procedures (see E.5).

The quality management system also includes the quality records identified in the procedures manuals, and personnel training and experience records.

All of the IT Infrastructure Library modules give guidance on developing procedures for IT service management.

The quality management system should be an integrated process, applied throughout the entire service lifecycle - thus ensuring that quality is "built in" rather than being implemented at the end of the development or delivery process. The emphasis should be on problem prevention, as opposed to correction after occurrence. The software lifecycle is covered in the **Software Lifecycle Support** module.

The quality system should incorporate a "feedback loop", so that assessments of services by IT Services and the customers are used to improve its quality.

E.3 Contract review [4.3]

To ensure that IT Services is able to provide quality services which meet its customer's requirements cost effectively, it should maintain procedures for contract review to ensure that:

* the requirements are adequately defined and documented

* IT Services has or will acquire the capability to meet contractual requirements

* any changes of requirement between for example, tender and contract or requirements specification and service level agreement are identified and resolved.

Contract in this context means the agreement with the actual, or planned, users of the IT service; in the case of a PRINCE/SSADM development this is likely to include:

* proposals or tenders to supply new or modified IT services

* the specification of requirements for new IT services or for modifications to existing services

* Service Level Agreements (see the **Service Level Management** module for a definition of an SLA).

It may be that no legal contract exists; for example in the case of an SLA between two parts of the same organization, or between government departments. However, the agreements noted above should be treated as though they were contracts for the purposes of the QMS and the standard (ISO 9001).

During the development or package procurement the IT Services Manager (with input from capacity management, cost management, availability management and planning unit as covered in the **Planning and Control for IT Services** module) should be involved in the specification of service requirements.

In particular the review should check that:

* the scope of the agreement and requirements are defined and documented

* potential risks and contingencies are identified

* any proprietary information is adequately protected

* any requirements which may have changed during discussions and negotiations are resolved

* IT Services has the capability to deliver the service contracted

* IT Services responsibility concerning any subcontracted work is defined

* the terminology is agreed by both parties

* the customer has the capability to meet its contractual obligations; for example, approving specifications, running acceptance tests.

Records of any such contract reviews should be maintained.

It may also be necessary to review underpinning contracts with suppliers to IT Services (see **Service Level Management** and **Third Party and Single Source Maintenance**).

The following items should also be considered for inclusion in any contract:

* acceptance criteria

* handling of any changes in the customer's requirement during the delivery of the service

* handling of any problems detected after acceptance, including any claims or complaints

* activities to be carried out by the customer, especially concerning requirements specification, delivery and acceptance

* any facilities or services to be provided by the customer

Annex E
Applying ISO 9001 to IT Services

* standards and procedures to be used
* any replication requirements (delivery or provision to multiple sites, for example).

The contract review activities, interfaces and communication within IT Services should be coordinated with the customer's organization, as appropriate (see **Customer Liaison**).

Records of contract reviews should be made and retained (see E.16).

E.4 Design control [4.4]

E.4.1 General [4.4.1]

The design control process covers both IT service design and development.

The objective of a software development or procurement project is not usually limited to developing or procuring software. It is usually intended to provide customers with a service which meets their requirements at an acceptable cost. Design, development and implementation of service delivery and support should be as much a part of the overall project as software development/procurement and installation, and hardware procurement and installation.

The **Software Lifecycle Support** module should be used to select the appropriate lifecycle model for the software components of the IT service.

As part of the design process it may be appropriate to convert the specification of requirements and any initial proposals made by the IT services supplier to the customer, into specifications for the service, its delivery and its control, as follows:

* the service specification: which defines the service to be provided
* the service delivery specification: which defines the means and methods used to deliver the specified service
* the quality control specification: which defines the procedures for evaluating and controlling the service and its delivery characteristics.

A configuration management (including change control) system is an essential component of the design control process. It provides a mechanism for identifying, controlling and tracking the versions of each configuration item (software, hardware, documentation) which affect the service being supplied to the customer. (See **Configuration Management** and **Change Management**).

It is particularly important that management assign responsibilities for service design, ensuring that those who contribute to the design are aware of their responsibilities for achieving service quality.

These responsibilities include:

* planning, preparation, validation, maintenance and control of the specifications (service, service delivery and quality control)

* specifying products and services to be procured for the service delivery process

* implementing design reviews for each phase

* validating the service delivery process against the service brief.

E.4.2 Design and development planning [4.4.2]

Reference should be made to the **Service Level Management** module and section 3 of the **Planning and Control for IT Services** module for a description of planning for new or modified services. The use of PRINCE and SSADM is recommended.

The following gives guidance on the service management products which need to be produced, together with their SSADM or PRINCE counterparts where applicable:

* service brief: equivalent to SSADM(v4) requirements catalogue (stage 1), where initial Service Level Requirements should be included (see the Managing Facilities Management module), together with the selected business system option (stage 2)

* service specification: equivalent to service requirements (see figure 4 in the **Service Level Management** module) or SSADM(v4) requirements specification, selected technical system option and technical environment description; also equivalent to Statement of Service Requirement (see **Managing Facilities Management** module)

* service delivery specification should include: a clear description of the service delivery characteristics which affect service performance; objectives or

Annex E
Applying ISO 9001 to IT Services

standards of acceptability for each; resource requirements detailing type and quantity of equipment and facilities necessary to fulfil the specification; number and skills of personnel required; reliance on sub-contractors for purchased products and services

* quality control specification should include: identification of the key activities in each process which will significantly influence the service; analysis of the activities to select those whose control will ensure service quality; definition of methods to evaluate the selected characteristics; means to influence or control the characteristics within specified limits.

The **Service Level Management** module includes guidance on key service items to be monitored.

The design approach will be similar irrespective of whether the IT service (as a whole or in part) is being provided in-house or contracted out (to a Facilities Management supplier for example); in the latter case a formal contract will be required.

Successful design and development planning depends on using suitably qualified personnel equipped with adequate resources. This is covered in the **Planning and Control for IT Services** module section 3.

Similarly the organizational and technical interfaces need to be defined (including those with customers and suppliers). These are likely to include: **Service Level Management**, **Capacity Management**, **Availability Management**, **Computer Operations Management**, **Network Services Management**, hardware and software suppliers. The modules covering these subjects (and the **Managing Facilities Management** and **Customer Liaison** modules) provide further guidance.

Service design and development planning must allow for service level reporting. This is addressed by **Service Level Management** and **Planning and Control for IT Services** (section 3). **Software Lifecycle Support** includes a section on how to use a lifecycle model to plan for service management.

The reader may also find sections 5.4 and 5.5 of ISO 9000 Part 3 helpful; these contain guidance on Development Planning and Quality Planning respectively (for software).

E.4.3 Design input [4.4.3]

The input to service design will normally be the customer's specification of requirements. This should comprise a complete, consistent and unambiguous set of functional and non-functional requirements necessary to satisfy the customer's need. Non-functional requirements may include, but are not limited to availability, reliability, usability, efficiency, maintainability, portability, contingency, safety, security, privacy, levels of support and constraints (See ISO 9126, **Service Level Management** and **Customer Liaison**).

The specification should be sufficiently precise for it to be used for validation during acceptance testing of the service (see **Testing an IT Service for Operational Use**).

The specification will either be provided by the customer or will be drawn up in close cooperation with the customer, whose approval should be obtained before the development stage is started. The specification is a controlled document (see E.5 below) and should be subject to configuration management (See **Configuration Management**).

In order for the customer's requirements specification to meet these criteria the following guidelines should be noted:

* a mechanism is needed for agreeing the requirements and approving changes (see **Change Management**)
* care is needed to prevent misunderstandings (definition of terms, explanations of background to requirements, for example)
* records of discussions should be kept.

E.4.4 Design output [4.4.4]

The service design process should be controlled by dividing it into a number of phases, each with clearly defined inputs and outputs. The required output from each service design phase should be defined and documented and the actual output verified to confirm that it:

* meets the relevant requirements
* contains or references acceptance criteria for subsequent phases
* conforms to appropriate standards, practices and conventions.

E.4.5 Design verification [4.4.5]

A plan should be prepared for verification of all design phase outputs at the end of each phase. The objective is to confirm that phase outputs meet the corresponding input requirements, through for example:

* development reviews at appropriate points
* tests and/or demonstrations.

Verification tests and any resultant, agreed actions should be recorded. Actions should be checked when complete. Only verified outputs should be submitted for configuration management and accepted for subsequent use.

The output from each phase should be reviewed for conformance against the service specification, service delivery specification and quality control specification. See **Testing an IT Service for Operational Use** module.

The design should be validated against the following criteria:

* consistency with the customer's requirements
* completeness of the service delivery process
* availability of resources to meet the service obligations
* conformance to any applicable standards or codes of practice
* availability of information to customers in the use of the service.

E.4.6 Design changes [4.4.6]

The **Change Management** and **Configuration Management** modules contain guidance on this subject.

Procedures are needed to identify, document, review and authorise any changes to items under configuration management.

These procedures should enable the validity of the change to be confirmed and any effect on other items assessed. They should also ensure that changes are notified to those concerned and that the records provide an audit trail to link changes to modified items.

This control should ensure that:

* the need for change is identified, verified and submitted for analysis and design

* changes to specifications are properly planned, documented, approved, implemented and recorded (see **Software Control and Distribution**)

* representatives of all affected functions participate in the approval process

* the impact is evaluated

* customers are informed of the effects of the change (see **Help Desk** and **Customer Liaison**).

E.5 Document control [4.5]

Procedures are needed to make sure that documents which require controlling are controlled. These will be documents which directly contribute to the quality of the IT service provided to the customer. They will include:

* policy and procedural documents: that is, those which describe the quality management system being applied (eg the quality manual, IT Services-wide standards and procedures, functional and service-based standards and procedures, and documents such as checklists and forms)

* planning documents: describing the planning and progress of all IT Services activities and its interactions with the customer (eg service design project plans and operations schedules - management products in PRINCE terms)

* contractual and "product" documents: describing an IT service and its components (eg specifications, test plans, service level agreements, service quality plans, user and operations manuals, purchase orders - technical products in PRINCE terms)

* quality records: which demonstrate achievement of the required quality and the effective operation of the quality management system - inspection and test results, change control records, sub-contractor assessments - quality products in PRINCE terms).

The document control policies and procedures should themselves be controlled documents, and a mechanism is needed to cover their issue and approval, changes to them and their eventual withdrawal (see **Change Management**).

Copies of documents held by users

A controlled copy of each current document sent to users will be kept by IT Services, but it is outside the scope of the IT Services quality management system to ensure that changes are applied to user manuals held by customers and that obsolete documents are removed from use.

Copies of documents issued for inspection

Where copies of IT Services' quality manual are issued for second or third party inspection they shall remain the responsibility of the Quality Manager, who will maintain a record of recipients, and recover the documents after the agreed retention period.

E.5.1 Document approval and issue [4.5.1]

Where documents are prepared or stored on computer (files produced by a word processing package for example) special attention needs to be paid to the approval, access, distribution and archiving to ensure that:

* the correct issue is available to the appropriate personnel
* obsolete documents are promptly removed from use and issue.

As stated earlier in the annex, it is desirable for IT Services to be involved in the development and maintenance of the applications software components of an IT service whenever possible. This should be considered when the document approval process is set up.

It may be appropriate for some controlled documents (service specifications, user guides for example) to be treated as configuration items, and recorded using the configuration management system, as described in the **Configuration Management** module.

E.5.2 Document changes/modifications [4.5.2]

Unless designated otherwise, changes must be reviewed and approved by the same functions/organizations which approved the original document. Hence any IT Services involvement (as discussed above) should be maintained - with consequent benefits to service quality.

The **Change Management** module also addresses this subject.

E.6 Purchasing [4.6]

E.6.1 General [4.6.1]

In order to provide its services, IT Services generally uses supplies, products and services purchased from external sources. For example: hardware and systems software, consumables, contract staff, user and staff training services, environmental products and services, hardware and software maintenance services, service specification services, equipment and tools to assist in the development and monitoring of its services, and perhaps application software development.

These items may be critical to the quality, cost, efficiency and/or safety of the IT services being supplied. Purchasing therefore needs the same level of planning, control and verification as "front line" IT Services activities. IT Services should invest time in establishing a good working relationship with its sub-contractors (see **Managing Supplier Relationships**). In this way a programme of continuing quality improvements will evolve and quality disputes be avoided or settled quickly.

Whether the products and services are for inclusion in an IT service, or to support quality management system activities, it is IT Services responsibility to ensure that the purchased products or services are of the required quality (that is, that they conform to the specified requirements). In particular, IT Services must ensure that:

* hardware and software configurations are capable of satisfying the service level requirements of the customer for whom they are intended

* all purchased hardware and software is the subject of inspection and acceptance tests by IT Services on receipt to ensure that it conforms to requirements. Records of these inspections and tests are retained. (See the IT Infrastructure Library **Testing an IT Service for Operational Use** and **Computer Installation and Acceptance** modules for guidance on product acceptance)

Note that:

* independent testing and certification schemes exist for a range of purchased products which may be components of a configuration to be supplied or for internal use, including, for example, language compilers and related products

Annex E
Applying ISO 9001 to IT Services

> * where software product are purchased for resale there should be a procedure to ensure that, where applicable, they are covered by appropriate licence agreements.
>
> Reference should also be made to the **Computer Installation and Acceptance** and **Managing Facilities Management** modules of the IT Infrastructure Library and to the CCTA Appraisal and Evaluation Library.

E.6.2 Assessment of sub-contractors [4.6.2]

In ISO 9001 terms, all the external suppliers of goods and services are sub-contractors.

In the context of IT service management, a sub-contractor is any individual or organization outside IT Services providing a product or service on a contractual basis (ie where a formal agreement is in place). Typically sub-contractors will include the provider of the hardware system maintenance service and any contract staff (trainers or technical specialists for example) used in the development or delivery of the IT service to the customer.

The quality management system should ensure that:

* prior to a contract award IT Services establishes that a sub-contractor is able to supply products and/or services of the required quality

* sub-contractor performance is assessed during the performance of the contract.

The performance of sub-contractors should be assessed by an appropriate method. The extent of any assessment will vary depending on the importance of the product or service to IT Services.

The assessment of potential sub-contractor performance could, for example, be:

* reference to records of past performance by the sub-contractor

* acceptance of a third party certification of the sub-contractor's quality management system; for example, certification to ISO 9001 (see Annex H)

* a second party audit by IT Services of the sub-contractor's quality management system.

Assessments of sub-contractor performance during the contract could, for example:

* be based on acceptance tests and an analysis of defects following installation (for hardware and software - see **Computer Installation and Acceptance** and **Testing an IT Service for Operational Use**)

* sub-contractor assessment of service quality and customer assessment of service quality followed by a comparison of the two (for services such as user training - note that if customer and subcontractor assessment of service quality is to be sought then this should be agreed in the contract, also that responsibility for obtaining the agreement and assessment should be defined in the relevant job descriptions)

* sample inspections of sub-contractor work or products (appropriate for consumables).

Records of pre-contract and in-contract assessments of sub-contractor performance should be retained as quality records (see E.16). IT Services should be able to demonstrate for management reviews and internal and external audits that the extent of the assessment required was considered, that the sub-contractor was selected using an appropriate procedure at an appropriate level of detail, and that sub-contractors are subjected to appropriate reassessment during the performance of a contract (and that this information is taken into account when placing subsequent contracts).

Procedures for sub-contractor assessment and control should be included in the appropriate procedure manual(s).

It is recommended that sub-contracted software developers and consultants (internal or external) involved in specifying, reviewing or auditing IT service management requirements should be expected to possess the ISEB IT Infrastructure Management (Service Management) certificate of proficiency.

See also **Third Party and Single Source Maintenance** and **Managing Supplier Relationships**.

E.6.3 Purchasing data [4.6.3]

When products or services are purchased a formal procedure should exist to ensure that all the necessary information is available to the sub-contractor and that IT

Services is able to establish that the sub-contractor can supply a product or service of the required quality. (The requirement here mirrors that in ISO 9001 4.3 - see E.3.)

This means that IT Services must specify sub-contract product and/or service requirements and ensure that contract reviews take place when appropriate.

Purchasing information supplied to the sub-contractor should include:

- * a description or specification of item(s) required
- * the quality requirements
- * quality assurance and verification requirements (eg acceptance criteria)
- * change control procedures.

If the customer (ie IT Services customer) is to be allowed to verify the conformity of sub-contracted products or services at cost then this requirement should be included in the purchasing documents and the contract. Customer involvement in sub-contractor assessment should only be depended on when it has specifically been requested and agreed.

See the CCTA Evaluation and Appraisal Library, **Testing an IT Service for Operational Use** and **Computer Installation and Acceptance**.

E.6.4 Verification of purchased product [4.6.4]

The service supplier is responsible for the verification and validation of any purchased products (including sub-contracted services). To help to achieve this it may be appropriate for IT Services to conduct design and other reviews of the sub-contractor's work. If this is to be the case, the requirement for it should be included in the contract, as should the requirements for any acceptance testing.

Where appropriate the customer should be given the opportunity to confirm whether a sub-contracted service (terminal installation for example) conforms to his requirement, although this does not absolve the IT Services of its responsibility to deliver an acceptable service to the customer.

E.7 Purchaser supplied product [4.7]

IT Services may be required to include products or services supplied by the customer (purchaser) in the IT service. This could be, for example, application software, existing terminals or a training course.

Responsibility for their quality is the responsibility of the customer, but IT services is still required to have procedures to verify, store, protect and maintain customer supplied products and verify customer supplied services. IT Services should not knowingly incorporate nonconforming products or services into an IT service to be supplied to the customer. Any defects or nonconformities should be recorded and reported to the customer and unsuitable products or services either rejected or allowed for as formal concessions against service requirements by the customer.

E.8 Product identification and traceability [4.8]

ISO 9001 requires that, where appropriate, IT Services should establish and maintain procedures for identifying a product at all stages of production and delivery and installation. This is so that any problems arising at any stage can be analyzed in order to find out the cause.

This requirement applies both to IT service development (design, development and installation in ISO 9001 terms) and IT service delivery (production and delivery in ISO 9001 terms). Identification and traceability requirements will be met if the guidance given in the IT Infrastructure Library **Configuration Management** module is followed for all components of an IT service (hardware, software, documentation, services, tools, test data, etc).

Ideally, the names of the personnel involved in each stage of the development or procurement of each component or delivery of an IT service should be recorded so that any problems or non-conformities arising from their performance may be addressed (eg by example, instruction or training).

Annex E
Applying ISO 9001 to IT Services

E.9 Process control [4.9]

E.9.1 General [4.9.1]

Process control applies both to the IT service development (ie design and installation) process and to the subsequent delivery process.

Use of PRINCE and SSADM will help to ensure that the development process is adequately controlled - as will the application of the guidance in the **Software Lifecycle Support**, **Computer Installation and Acceptance**, **Planning and Control for IT Services**, **Configuration Management**, **Testing an IT Service for Operational Use** modules of the IT Infrastructure Library.

The requirement to control the IT service delivery process is addressed by this module, and other IT Infrastructure Library modules such as **Service Level Management**, **Computer Operations Management**, **Network Services Management** and **Management of Local Processors and Terminals**.

E.9.2 Special processes [4.9.2]

ISO 9000 requires that special attention is paid to processes in which control is particularly important to product or service quality. For IT services this may require the inclusion of controls, in-process checks or metrics to allow measurement during service delivery.

E.10 Inspection and testing [4.10]

IT Services policies and procedures should include requirements for inspection and/or testing at three stages in the life of an IT service:

* on receipt of any purchased product or service - this will include the delivery of minor items such as consumables, minor software changes or hardware configuration items, as well as major items such as hardware configurations or applications software systems; ISO 9001 refers to this as *receiving inspection and testing*, it includes, for example, operational acceptance testing

* during IT service development or delivery; *in-process inspection and testing*

> * prior to final release to the customer; *final inspection and testing* - for service development this requirement includes system testing, for service delivery this requirement includes, for example, a review of printouts to ensure that they are complete.

E.10.1 Receiving inspection and testing [4.10.1]

All hardware, software, consumables and services (such as training or maintenance) purchased by IT Services for inclusion in a configuration or IT service to be supplied to a customer, or equipment and tools purchased to assist in the development or delivery of IT services, must be verified and/or validated (as appropriate) upon receipt.

The level of receiving inspection and testing will depend on the level of confidence in the supplier. (As a minimum, all deliveries or hardware or consumables should be inspected for type and quantity, and for evidence of transit damage or deterioration due to poor storage conditions.)

More guidance on receiving inspection and testing by IT Services is given in **Computer Installation and Acceptance**, **Testing an IT Service for Operational Use** and **Computer Operations Management** modules.

Software Control and Distribution (section 3) addresses the need for checks before adding software to the definitive software library.

Procedures are required to ensure that any urgent changes are properly dealt with, in accordance with ISO 9001 paragraph 4.10.1.2. The **Change Management** module includes guidance on "Urgent Changes" and the **Software Control and Distribution** module on "Urgent Releases".

E.10.2 In-process inspection and testing [4.10.2]

In the context of service delivery, in-process inspection and testing is performed by both IT Services and the customer.

IT Services should:

> * measure and verify the key processes affecting delivery (these will have been identified during the preparation of the service quality plan)
>
> * encourage continuous self-inspection by IT Services service delivery personnel
>
> * provide a means of assessing the IT service at the point of delivery to the customer.

The modules on **Service Level Management** (section 3 and Annex F), **Help Desk**, **Problem Management**, **Availability Management** and **Capacity Management** all provide guidance.

The customer's assessment is the ultimate measure of the quality of a service. IT Services therefore needs to institute an ongoing assessment and measurement of customer satisfaction, seeking positive as well as negative reactions.

This is addressed by the **Customer Liaison**, **Help Desk** and **Managing Local Processors and Terminals** modules.

E.10.3 Final inspection and testing [4.10.3]

These requirements are covered by the **Computer Installation and Acceptance**, **Testing an IT Service for Operational Use**, **Computer Operations Management** and **Software Control and Distribution** modules.

This process also needs to check that any equipment being provided to the customer is suitable for its purpose and that written instructions are given, as required, for its use.

E.10.4 Inspection and test records [4.10.4]

It should be noted that inspection and test records are quality records and therefore subject to ISO 9001 paragraph 4.16 (see paragraph E.16 of this annex). The Configuration Management Database should record inspection and test status (see the **Configuration Management** module).

E.11 Inspection, measuring and test equipment [4.11]

ISO 9001 requires that all items of equipment used in test, verification and replication processes are controlled and, where appropriate, calibrated.

Inspection, measuring and test equipment in the context of IT Services Equipment includes such things as software, operations (system, installation and acceptance) tests and checklists as well as hardware.

IT Services should use tools, facilities and techniques in order to make the quality system guidelines of ISO 9001 effective. Such tools, facilities and techniques can be effective for management purposes as well as for service development and delivery. IT Services should improve these tools and techniques as required.

The use of monitoring tools (response time, throughput for example) is covered by the **Service Level Management** and **Capacity Management** modules. Reference should also be made to **Computer Installation and Acceptance**, **Testing an IT Service for Operational Use** and **Computer Operations Management**.

E.12 Inspection and test status [4.12]

ISO 9001 requires that it must be possible to determine the inspection and test status of IT services and service components at all times during service development and delivery. In particular, it should be possible to identify the inspection authority or individual responsible for verifying that a service or service component conforms to the requirement at a given stage of service development or delivery. This means that if problems are discovered later then the causes can be traced and analyzed.

The responsibility for the final release of a service or product must be defined.

The **Configuration Management** and **Software Lifecycle Support** modules explain how the status of each component of the service (software, manual etc) is identified, recorded and audited.

E.13 Control of non-conforming product [4.13]

Products or services which do not conform to specified requirements need to be identified in order to prevent their inadvertent use or installation. Procedures must exist for the control, review and disposition of any nonconforming product or service. As soon as any indication occurs that materials, components, products or services (including purchased products and services) do not or may not meet the specified requirements then these procedures must be followed. The procedures should cover identification, segregation, review, disposition, documentation and prevention of recurrence.

Identification and reporting of non-conforming services or products (i.e. where the delivered service does not match the customer's requirement) is the responsibility of each individual in IT Services.

This subject is addressed by the **Service Level Management**, **Help Desk**, **Problem Management**, **Configuration Management**, **Change Management** and **Testing an IT Service for Operational Use** modules.

Annex E
Applying ISO 9001 to IT Services

E.14 Corrective action [4.14]

A major objective of the quality management system should be to remove the causes of non-conforming services and products.

When a non-conformity is detected, action should be taken to record, analyze and correct it. This will frequently be a two-stage process: immediate action to satisfy the short-term needs of the customer followed by an evaluation of the root cause to determine and apply the corrective action needed to prevent recurrence.

More detailed guidance on appropriate procedures is given in the **Problem Management**, **Help Desk** and **Change Management** modules of the IT Infrastructure Library.

E.15 Handling, storage, packaging and delivery [4.15]

Each product (eg terminals, printers, diskettes and other consumables, manuals) supplied by or to IT Services must be handled, stored and packed in an appropriate way in order to avoid damage or deterioration. Appropriate standards, and procedures and responsibilities should be defined and documented.

E.16 Quality records [4.16]

Quality records are maintained in order to demonstrate achievement of the required quality and the effective operation of the quality system; in particular, to:

* establish that the service is developed and maintained in accordance with the customer's requirements
* record actions taken, changes made, defects found etc, for reference purposes
* provide the data necessary for review of quality related activities and identification of corrective action
* demonstrate effective operation of the quality system.

Examples include: configuration management records, acceptance test records, help desk logs, maintenance call records.

E.17 Internal quality audits [4.17]

Internal quality audits are required by ISO 9001 to determine whether or not the quality management system is being followed and whether or not it is effective. In particular whether:

* the quality management system documentation meets the requirements of the standard and adequately defines the needs of the business
* the documented procedures are practical, understood and followed
* the training is adequate.

The quality management system must include procedures for planning and carrying out internal quality audits.

The timing and frequency of audits will vary depending on the importance of a particular part of the system.

Audits should be carried out by responsible persons independent of the activity being audited.

The results of audits should be documented and include:

* the deficiencies found
* the corrective action required
* the time agreed for the corrective action to be carried out
* the person responsible for carrying out the corrective action.

The persons conducting audits (which include external auditors) must be properly trained to carry out the task objectively and effectively in accordance with ISO 10011 "Guide to quality systems auditing".

General guidance on quality audits is given in the QMS Audit volume of the QML. Specific guidance in relation to IT service management functions is given in section 5 of each IT Infrastructure Library module.

E.18 Training [4.18]

Training for personnel at all levels and in all functions within IT Services is central to the achievement of quality; that is, both specific training to perform assigned tasks and general training to heighten quality awareness and to influence attitudes.

IT Services should therefore develop procedures which enable it to:

* identify the skill, knowledge and qualifications required to carry out tasks
* determine the training needs of the individuals to be assigned to carry out those tasks
* plan and carry out appropriate specific training (this may be provided either internally or externally)
* plan and carry out general quality awareness programmes
* retain records of education, qualification, skills, training and experience which can be used to help to judge the training requirements of personnel.

Particular attention should be paid to the selection and training of new personnel and of personnel transferred to new assignments.

Further guidance on quality training is given in the Quality Training volume of the QML.

E.19 Servicing [4.19]

ISO 9001 requires that, where servicing is required by the contract, IT Services should have procedures to ensure that the servicing meets the requirements. In the context of IT Services, servicing means the maintenance (corrective, perfective or adaptive) of service configuration items.

The scope of the maintenance service will be determined by the customer's requirements. Further guidance on SLAs and contracts with suppliers is given in **Service Level Management** and **Managing Supplier Relationships** modules.

The **Availability Management** module gives guidance on the specification of serviceability requirements and on contractual monitoring of serviceability. Refer to the **Change Management** module for guidance on procedures to control changes and, in particular, paragraph 3.1.2.12 on change review.

E.20 Statistical techniques [4.20]

Statistical techniques can help to design and improve methods of data collection and analysis, and to apply the results of analyses to service and process improvement.

In order to improve the quality of its services, IT Services should develop quantitative measures of both IT service quality and IT service development quality.

Service quality measurement

In order to improve the quality of its services, IT Services should collect, analyze and act on quantitative measures of service quality. Specifically, these measures should be used to:

* identify and report performance on a regular basis
* take remedial action if metric levels deteriorate or fall below established target levels
* establish specific service improvement goals.

As a minimum, the metrics developed and used should allow IT Services to identify and classify reported incidents from both the customer's and IT Services' viewpoint.

Service development measurement

IT Services should also collect and analyze quantitative measures of the development and installation process to determine:

* how well the IT service design and installation process is being carried out in terms of milestones and in-process quality objectives being met on schedule
* how effective the IT service design and installation process is at reducing the probability that faults are introduced or that any faults go undetected (this should include measures of the effectiveness of operational acceptance testing, and where appropriate, measures to feed information back to Application Development or Application Maintenance.

Reference should also be made to the **Planning and Control for IT Services** module (and the role of the IT Planning Unit) and the Quality Techniques volume of the QML.

Annex F. How the ITIL functions and modules relate to ISO 9000

This annex discusses how the requirements of ISO 9001 affect each of the IT service management functions defined in the IT Infrastructure Library. The annex should be read in conjunction with the standard (ISO 9001).

The IT service management functions considered, addressed in alphabetical order for ease of reference, are:

* Availability Management
* Capacity Management
* Change Management
* Computer Installation and Acceptance Management (see **Computer Installation and Acceptance**)
* Computer Operations Management (including Unattended Operations)
* Configuration Management
* Contingency Planning
* Cost Management (see **Cost Management for IT Services**)
* Customer Liaison
* Help Desk Management (see **Help Desk**)
* IT Services Organization
* Management of Local Processors and Terminals
* Managing Facilities Management
* Network Services Management
* Planning and Control for IT Services
* Problem Management
* Service Level Management
* Software Control and Distribution Management (see **Software Control and Distribution**)
* Software Lifecycle Support
* Supplier Management (see **Managing Supplier Relationships**)
* Testing an IT Service for Operational Use
* Third Party and Single Source Maintenance.

For each function the relevant requirements of the standard are discussed under the ISO 9001 paragraph number and title. For example, *4.1.2.2 Verification resources and personnel* where 4.1.2.2 refers to paragraph 4.1.2.2 of ISO 9001.

F.1 Availability Management

F.1.1 ISO 9001

4.1.2.2   *Verification resources and personnel*

Where availability requirements for IT services have been defined, there will be a need for "adequate resources and trained personnel". This is necessary for service design, development and delivery. For example, design verification (paragraph 4.4.5), in-process inspection and testing (4.10.2) and final inspection and testing (4.10.3) need to be undertaken by suitably trained staff.

4.3   *Input to contract review*

The Availability Management function should ensure that availability requirements are adequately defined and documented, and accurately reflect the customer's needs. They should also ensure that IT Services has the capability to meet the requirements.

4.4.3   *Design input*

Paragraph 4.4.3 requires that "design input requirements relating to the product" be identified and documented. It is likely that design inputs will include availability requirements or constraints.

4.4.4   *Design output*

Paragraph 4.4.4 requires that design output shall: "(b) contain or reference acceptance criteria", "(d) identify those characteristics of the design that are crucial to the safe and proper functioning of the product".

Availability requirements will normally be specified (see paragraph 4.3) and form part of the user and/or operational acceptance criteria and, because of the potential effect on service quality (of this and other services), these are likely to be amongst those characteristics which are crucial to the proper functioning of the service.

4.4.5   *Design verification*

The Availability Management function is responsible for ensuring that the designs for a service will meet the availability requirements, using the techniques given in Section 3 of the module.

Annex F
How the ITIL functions and modules relate to ISO 9000

4.6.1 *Purchasing - general*

The service supplier is responsible for ensuring that any purchased product or service (systems software, packaged software, hardware, communications service) conforms to the requirements specified in the service design. In particular, where reliability requirements have been specified (see paragraph 4.6.3 in this section), the Availability Management function is responsible for checking conformance of the individual products.

4.6.2 *Assessment of sub-contractors*

If contract or other external staff are needed to assist with the establishment, review or modification of the Availability Management function, or its day-to-day running, then their ability to meet the requirements of the job should be verified using the guidelines of this paragraph and section 3 of the module.

4.6.3 *Purchasing data*

Availability and reliability requirements should be included in any Operational Requirement or Invitation to Tender issued. Where an Availability Management function exists it should contribute to the definition of these requirements (as described in the module) and the drafting and negotiation of contractual agreements with external suppliers.

4.6.4 *Verification of purchased product*

The service supplier is responsible for ensuring that purchased product meets the specified availability/reliability requirements, by, for example, checking the product (reference number, modification level etc) against the order, or in extreme cases checking the results of reliability tests on the external supplier's premises before delivery.

4.9.2 *Special processes*

The software/service design and construction process comes under this heading. This means that continuous monitoring of live services is required to ensure that they meet their availability requirements. The monitoring requirements for a service should be set out in the service quality plan, and appropriate procedures established to ensure that availability requirements are met.

The **Availability Management** module describes methods of calculating availability (Annex B), techniques for analysing availability (Annex F) and data items to be recorded for each event which occurs which is not part of the normal operation of an IT service (Annex H). Section 3 covers appropriate procedures.

4.10.2 *In-process inspection and testing*

This paragraph requires that any incoming product released for urgent production purposes is suitably recorded as such, so that it can be immediately recalled in the event of problems.

This applies to replacement or repaired hardware items (terminals for example) or software updates, whose reliability can be tested only to a limited extent before release into production.

4.10.4 *Inspection and test records*

Availability management monitoring data and reports are considered as inspection and test records which show compliance with the defined service level requirements. They are also quality records, to which paragraph 4.16 applies.

4.11 *Inspection measuring and test equipment*

"Equipment" in this context also means any software tools used for availability management (see section 7 of the module).

4.14 *Corrective action*

The Availability Management function is responsible for corrective action where availability requirements are not being met.

4.16 *Quality records*

Quality records comprise all availability testing and monitoring data (including the records of any testing or calibration of availability management tools), audit reports, training records and quality cost reports.

4.17 *Internal quality audits*

Any Availability Management function should be the subject of internal quality audits to establish whether availability management activities comply with the published procedures and to determine the effectiveness of the quality system (see section 5 of the module).

Annex F
How the ITIL functions and modules relate to ISO 9000

4.18 *Training*

Because availability management activities affect service quality, personnel performing availability management tasks need to be "qualified on the basis of appropriate education, training and/or experience". See sections 3 and 5 of the module.

4.20 *Statistical techniques*

Statistical techniques are a fundamental means of verifying the acceptability of the processes which are used to design a service to meet the customer's availability requirements. They are also used to verify product characteristics and to verify that the overall service satisfies the customer's requirement.

The annexes to the module show how such techniques can be used.

F.2 Capacity Management

F.2.1 ISO 9001

4.3 *Input to contract review*

A critical factor in successful capacity management (and consequently delivering a service which is acceptable to the customer) is the definition of the capacity requirements - data volumes, number of users, transaction throughput, transaction profile, distribution, performance requirements, etc.

Sub-paragraphs (a) and (b) are directly applicable to this process in that they call for the requirements to be defined and documented (in the service specification or SLA) - and then reviewed in order to resolve any differences from those specified in the tender/proposal submitted to the customer.

Sub-paragraph (c) requires the service supplier to review the specification/SLA to establish that he has the capability to meet the requirements.

This implies that the service supplier must be aware of the likely capacity requirements for the proposed service, and their likely impact on existing services. This does not mean that a Capacity Management function is an essential part of a QMS since experienced staff should be able to provide some estimated requirements and effects without recourse to a Capacity Management Database (CMDB). However, to be confident of offering a quality service a capacity planning function is clearly highly desirable.

The module (section 6) gives examples of other benefits such as: customer relations, appropriate service levels, confident forecasts, anticipation of problems.

4.4.3 *Design input*

This paragraph requires that "design inputs relating to the product" be identified and documented. It is likely that design inputs will include performance requirements, capacity constraints or targets, and possibly some assumptions which will need to be agreed with the customer.

4.4.4 *Design output*

This paragraph requires that design output shall: contain or reference acceptance criteria (sub-paragraph b), and identify those characteristics of the design that are crucial to the safe and proper functioning of the product (d). Performance and capacity requirements will normally be specified (see paragraph 4.3) and form part of the operational acceptance criteria. Because of the potential effect on service quality (of this and other services), performance and capacity are likely to be amongst those characteristics which are crucial to the proper functioning of the service.

4.4.5 *Design verification*

This paragraph requires the service supplier, using the Capacity Management function or otherwise, to verify the design output. This could be achieved by: running performance and capacity tests; further sizing calculations; comparisons with other similar services, etc.

4.6.3 *Purchasing data*

Capacity Management should be involved in the preparation of purchasing documents for any additional items such as hardware, systems software, performance consultancy services.

4.7 *Purchaser supplied product*

Capacity Management may need to verify that purchaser supplied equipment (customer's PCs or Local Area Network) is capable of meeting the specified performance and capacity requirements. However, it should be noted that verification by the service supplier does not absolve the customer of the responsibility to provide acceptable product.

Annex F
How the ITIL functions and modules relate to ISO 9000

4.9.2 *Special processes*

The theoretical nature of capacity planning means that the results of this part of IT service development (whether sufficient disc controllers have been allocated, for example) cannot be fully verified by inspection and testing of the service.

This paragraph therefore requires that the service supplier continuously monitors service performance to ensure that the customer's requirements are being met.

4.10.2 *In-process inspection and testing*

As part of the service commissioning process the Capacity Management function will need to monitor performance and capacity utilisation to establish product conformance to specified requirements, and identify non-conforming product.

4.11 *Inspection, measuring and test equipment*

This paragraph applies to all capacity management tools: performance monitoring software, network management hardware and software, communications line monitors, etc. The control, calibration and inspection are the responsibility of the Capacity Management function.

4.14 *Corrective action*

All parts of this paragraph are relevant but in particular the following three aspects.

(a) The reasons for failure to conform to performance or capacity requirements should be investigated by the Capacity Management function, and corrective action needs to be taken to prevent recurrence.

A potential cause is over-use of the service: in other words the customer usage (volume of data stored, number of users, transaction throughput) exceeds the originally agreed service specification or SLA. In this case, procedures will be needed for managing the demand (as described in the module) or for returning to the contract review stage in order to revise the customer's requirements.

(b) Capacity Management also needs to use the results of monitoring and feedback through the Help Desk and other sources of complaints to detect and eliminate potential performance and capacity problems, as discussed in the preceding paragraph.

| | | (c) | Note that preventative actions initiated to deal with problems should be "to a level corresponding to the risks encountered". |

4.16 *Quality records*

This paragraph requires the service supplier to maintain records of test results, performance monitoring and testing/monitoring equipment calibration.

4.17 *Internal quality audits*

Capacity Management will need to be audited for compliance with the QMS if the function exists.

4.18 *Training*

This paragraph requires that "Personnel performing specific tasks shall be qualified on the basis of appropriate education, training and/or experience". The requirements for Capacity Management are set out in section 3 of the module.

4.19 *Servicing*

The service supplier needs to assess the performance and capacity implications of any system maintenance activities - upgrading of software or hardware items which provide greater functionality but could impair system performance, for example.

4.20 *Statistical techniques*

This paragraph applies, given the nature of capacity management. Annex B of the module provides guidance.

F.2.2 ISO 9004-2

Paragraph 4.1 applies in particular. It specifies that the requirements of a service need to be defined in terms of characteristics which "...may not always be observable by the customer, but directly affect service performance...". Examples of characteristics given include capacity.

F.3 Change Management

F.3.1 ISO 9001

4.4.6 *Design changes*

This paragraph states the basic rule which should apply to any Change Management function, in order for a quality service to be maintained.

Annex F
How the ITIL functions and modules relate to ISO 9000

4.5.1 *Document approval and issue*
4.5.2 *Document changes/modifications*

Any procedures within the change management system concerning documents (customer's requirements specification, Service Level Agreement, service specification, for example) will need to comply with these paragraphs.

4.9.1 *Process control - general*

Change management normally involves changes to the service after operational use by the customer has started. The introduction of changes therefore requires careful control, as stated in this paragraph, if service quality is to be preserved.

For example: all items to be presented for installation into the live environment must be registered in a configuration management system and brought under configuration management control. Procedures should be defined to control the installation of new or modified Configuration Items (and also the removal of Configuration Items). The **Change Management** module describes procedures for authorising and implementing IT infrastructure changes, and **Testing Software for Operational Use** covers the control of the movement of components into and out of independent testing environments. The **Software Control and Distribution** module covers registration for software, **Computer Installation and Acceptance** covers the actions required for hardware, and **Network Services Management** does the same for communications equipment. The **Management of Local Processors and Terminals** covers the actions required for terminals and small computers.

4.12 *Inspection and test status*

The change management system must take into account the requirements of this paragraph concerning the identification of the status of configuration items, through all development stages, and the arrangements for release of non-conforming product.

4.13.1 *Non-conformity review and disposition*

The change management system should take account of the requirements of this paragraph.

4.14 *Corrective action*

The change management system should be used to cover the requirements of sub-paragraphs (d) and (e).

| | 4.16 | *Quality records* |

All change records count as quality records and are therefore subject to this paragraph.

| | 4.17 | *Internal quality audits* |

The Change Management function should be subject to internal quality audits to establish whether change management activities comply with the established procedures and to determine the effectiveness of the quality system.

| | 4.18 | *Training* |

Change management activities affect service quality. Personnel performing change management tasks should be "qualified on the basis of appropriate education, training and/or experience", as recommended in section 3 of the module.

F.4 Computer Installation and Acceptance

F.4.1 ISO 9001

| | 4.1.2.2 | *Verification resources and personnel* |

"Verification activities shall include inspection, test and monitoring of ... installation." Verification requirements for computer installation should be identified, adequate resources provided, and trained personnel assigned.

| | 4.6.1 | *Purchasing - general* |

This paragraph states the service provider's responsibility for ensuring that purchased products and services (hardware, software, installation services) conform to specified requirements.

| | 4.6.3 | *Purchasing data* |

Products and services being purchased need to be defined in accordance with this paragraph. An approval process for purchasing documents is also needed.

| | 4.6.4 | *Verification of purchased product* |

IT services should always include a clause in an Invitation to Tender or contract which affords it the right - either as the purchaser or the purchaser's agent - to verify upon receipt that purchased product conforms to the specified requirements. It may also wish to reserve the right to verify at source where this is considered appropriate.

Annex F
How the ITIL functions and modules relate to ISO 9000

It should be noted, however, that verification at the sub-contractor's (system supplier's) plant is not sufficient to satisfy the requirements of this ISO 9001 clause. Evidence of effective control of quality by a sub-contractor requires long-term monitoring of the quality of the supplier's products, a second party assessment of the supplier's quality system by the IT service organization, or third party certification (i.e. ISO 9001) by an accredited body.

4.7 *Purchaser supplied product*

Where the customer organization supplies hardware or software for use in service provision then the IT service organization must establish and maintain procedures for the verification, storage and maintenance of this product. In this situation, it is the customer's responsibility to provide acceptable products. However if IT Services' verification shows such products to be unacceptable the customer must be informed and remedial action discussed.

4.9.1 *Process control - general*

The installation of computer equipment and software is a process which directly affects the quality of the service. The IT service organization must therefore identify and plan the installation processes and ensure that they are carried out under controlled conditions as defined in this paragraph.

4.10.1 *Receiving inspection and testing*

The requirements and acceptance criteria for any purchased product should have been defined either during a full study or during preparation of an Operational Requirement. These should include procedures and criteria for receiving inspection: for example, have all the items been supplied? to the correct specification and version number? are they in good condition?. The quality plan or procedures should also include any appropriate acceptance tests for the purchased items (see section 3 of the module and CCTA Model Agreements).

4.10.3 *Final inspection and testing*

Final inspection and testing prior to the introduction of the computer service requires that all receiving inspection and testing has been carried out, and that the results of the inspection and testing of the overall system satisfy the acceptance criteria.

	4.11	*Inspection, measuring and test equipment*
		Any inspection, measuring and test equipment (hardware or software monitors for example) are subject to the requirements of this paragraph.
	4.12	*Inspection and test status*
		It must be possible to identify the inspection and test status of any purchased, customer-supplied or in-house products, and determine whether or not the product conforms to the specified requirements. Only products which have passed the required inspections and tests should be used.
	4.13	*Control of nonconforming product*
		This paragraph requires that any product items (hardware of software) which has been found not to conform to requirements be prevented from inadvertent use or installation.
	4.16	*Quality records*
		All quality records (such as inspection and test records) need to be retained.

F.5 Computer Operations Management

This section also addresses "Unattended Operations" which can be considered a special case of Computer Operations Management.

F.5.1 ISO 9001

	4.9.1	*Process control - general*
		Work Instructions are needed which define the tasks Operations staff need to carry out in order to deliver a quality service to the customer. These will have been specified during the service development phase, but will typically include: start/end of day procedures, loading magnetic media, stationery changes, data back-ups, security procedures.
	4.9.2	*Special processes*
		Similarly Work Instructions are needed to cover those aspects of the service which cannot be fully tested during service development. Typically these will apply to performance (throughput, response time, batch run-times) and availability, and will explain to staff how these are to be monitored and the actions to be taken where there is a risk of the customer's requirements not being met.

Annex F
How the ITIL functions and modules relate to ISO 9000

4.10.1 *Receiving inspection and testing*

"Incoming product" in this context would include: consumables (magnetic media, stationery, ribbons etc), replacement equipment (PCs, printers if these have been repaired off-site), software updates and "patches".

4.10.2 *In-process inspection and testing*

This paragraph requires that inspection and/or testing, as appropriate, is carried out to check that the processes referred to by paragraphs 4.9.1 and 4.9.2 are successful.

4.10.3 *Final inspection and testing*

Products to which this paragraph would apply include: printed output (reports, letters), job journals, magnetic media.

4.10.4 *Inspection and test records*

These include the monitoring, control and inspection/test records required by paragraphs 4.9.2, 4.10.1, 4.10.2 and 4.10.3.

4.11 *Inspection, measuring and test equipment*

This applies to any hardware or software used for inspection, measuring or test. Any hardware monitors may need to be subject to a calibration programme, in order to demonstrate their continued accuracy, whereas the validation of software tools would probably only need to repeated if the software was changed in some way (new version for example).

4.12 *Inspection and test status*

This applies to any defective hardware or software item. The requirement will normally be satisfied by the use of a configuration management system.

F.6 Configuration Management

F.6.1 ISO 9001

A Configuration Management (CM) system, particularly if supported by software tools, will help the IT service organization comply with many of the requirements of ISO 9001. This section therefore highlights which ISO 9001 paragraphs a CM system needs to address in particular.

4.4.6 *Design changes*

Changes to the overall service design will require changes to specification documents. If these are Configuration Items (CIs) then the CM system can be used to ensure conformance with this paragraph.

Note that section 2 of the module recommends that a single CM system is used to control components in both live and development environments.

4.5.1 *Document approval and issue*
4.5.2 *Document changes/modifications*

The CM system can and should be used for the control of documents (specifications, manuals for example) in accordance with these paragraphs - as suggested in section 3 of the module.

4.7 *Purchaser supplied product*

Similarly the status (verified, defective etc) of product supplied by the customer (PCs, printers, software) can be recorded by the CM system.

4.8 *Product identification and traceability*

This clause applies to all items which constitute the service delivered to the customer, including: purchased products such as software and hardware (for which serial and version numbers should be recorded), in-house developed software products, service outputs such as reports, screens, payable orders, cheques etc. Guidance on labelling is given in section 3 of the CM module.

[Software product is defined as a complete set of computer programs, procedures and associated documentation and data designated for delivery to a user (ISO 9000-3 paragraph 3.2)]

The batch traceability referred to in the second paragraph is particularly relevant to the distribution of software (refer to the **Software Control and Distribution** module).

4.9.1 *Process control - general*

This paragraph requires the service supplier to identify and plan those service development and delivery processes which directly affect quality.

CM is directly relevant to the introduction of new CIs. All items to be presented for acceptance (installation) into the live environment must be registered in a CM system and brought under CM control. Procedures should be defined to control the introduction (installation) of new or modified

CIs (and also the removal of CIs). The **Change Management** module describes procedures for authorizing and implementing IT infrastructure changes, and **Testing Software for Operational Use** covers the control of the movement of components into and out of independent testing environments. The **Software Control and Distribution** module covers registration for software, **Computer Installation and Acceptance** covers the actions required for hardware, and **Network Services Management** does the same for communications equipment. The **Management of Local Processors and Terminals** covers the actions required for terminals and small computers.

4.10.1.2 *Receiving inspection and testing (sub-paragraph 2)*

The CM system should be used for recording the release of incoming product for urgent production purposes in accordance with this sub-paragraph. This applies to both urgent hardware and software items.

4.10.2 *In-process inspection and testing*

The CM system should be used to satisfy the identification requirements of this paragraph.

4.10.4 *Inspection and test records*

Similarly the CM system may be used to keep records to demonstrate that individual CIs have been inspected or tested.

4.12 *Inspection and test status*

Inspection and test status of CIs should be recorded in the CM database in accordance with this paragraph.

4.13 *Control of nonconforming product*

The CM system can be used to meet the requirements of this paragraph.

4.14 *Corrective action*

The use of the CM system should help ensure that controls are applied to check that corrective actions are taken; for example by producing reports of CIs marked as nonconforming.

4.16 *Quality records*

Quality records may be treated as CIs and controlled using the CM system.

A CM system which follows the recommendations given in the module will hold records which demonstrate the effective operation of the quality system, thereby satisfying many of the requirements of this paragraph.

4.17 *Internal quality audits*

Any CM function should be a subject of internal quality audits to check that its activities comply with the established procedures and to determine the effectiveness of the quality system, as recommended in section 5 of the module.

4.18 *Training*

CM activities affect service quality. CM personnel need to be "qualified on the basis of appropriate education, training and/or experience". Sections 3 and 5 of the module provide further guidance.

F.7 Contingency planning

F.7.1 ISO 9001

4.3 *Contract review*

Contingency requirements for a service should be established during the requirements specification stage, and reviewed prior to final service level agreement, in accordance with this paragraph.

4.4 *Design control*

Preparing contingency plans to meet the agreed contingency requirements should be treated as a service design activity and therefore subject to design control procedures.

4.5 *Document control*

Similarly, service contingency plans should be subject to document control procedures.

4.6 *Purchasing*

Where external services are to be purchased as part of a contingency plan, their procurement should be carried out in accordance with defined procedures.

In particular, it is recommended that the customer should be involved in the verification of products and services procured for a contingency plan.

| | 4.15 | *Handling, storage, packaging and delivery* |

This paragraph applies to product which has been purchased, installed or stored as part of a contingency plan.

| | 4.17 | *Internal quality audits* |

Any contingency planning function should be a subject of internal quality audits to establish whether its activities comply with the established procedures and to determine the effectiveness of the quality system, as recommended in section 5 of the module.

F.8 Cost Management

F.8.1 ISO 9001

| | 4.3 | *Contract review* |

Contract review should include ensuring that the Service Management organization can provide the required service(s) at the agreed cost(s)/charge(s). Costs and charges must be clearly defined and documented.

| | 4.4.3 | *Design input* |

The charges which the customer expects to pay for the service is an important input requirement and therefore subject to this paragraph.

| | 4.4.4 | *Design output* |

The service to be provided to the customer may incorporate a charging mechanism which reflects the costs to the service provider (cost of hardware, software, maintenance, consumables, media, communications lines etc). The mechanism to be used (processing units, input/output transfers, main/disc storage, etc) will be a design output and therefore subject to this paragraph.

| | 4.4.6 | *Design changes* |

The cost and charging implications of design changes should be considered and approved (costs need not be disclosed to the customer).

| | 4.9.2 | *Special processes* |

Whether costing and charging algorithms:

- * adequately cover the costs of delivering the service
- * meet the customer's cost requirements
- * is unlikely to be verifiable until the customer is using the service for live work.

The charging method, assuming algorithms are used, is therefore a "special process", and the continuous monitoring described in this paragraph applies.

4.17   *Internal quality audits*

Any Cost Management function should be a subject of internal quality audits to establish whether its activities comply with the established procedures and to determine the effectiveness of the quality system. See section 5 of the module.

4.20   *Statistical techniques*

This paragraph applies, given that statistical techniques are normally used to derive charging algorithms.

F.9 Customer Liaison

F.9.1 ISO 9001

4.4.1   *Design control - general*

Those responsible for Customer Liaison have an important role to play in verifying the design of the service in order to ensure that the specified requirements are met. They should make sure that the requirements are interpreted correctly (that the customer's needs are understood) and that the service will fully satisfy those needs.

4.4.5   *Design verification*

Similarly those responsible for Customer Liaison need to be involved in the service design verification process, which is likely to include design reviews. They may also decide to involve customer staff, if appropriate.

4.10.3   *Final inspection and testing*

They have a similarly important role in establishing whether the service meets the customer's requirements, before the customer starts using it.

4.14   *Corrective action*

Customer Liaison staff should be involved in the service supplier's procedures for corrective action: for example, dealing with customer complaints; ensuring that corrective actions are effective, in terms of improving the quality of service to the customer.

4.16   *Quality records*

Quality records include all customer survey questionnaires.

4.17 *Internal quality audits*

Any Customer Liaison function should be a subject of internal quality audits to establish whether its activities comply with the established procedures and to determine the effectiveness of the quality system. See section 5 of the module.

4.18 *Training*

Those responsible for Customer Liaison activities need to be "qualified on the basis of appropriate education, training and/or experience". Sections 3 and 5 of the module, and the Annexes, provide guidance.

4.20 *Statistical techniques*

The module shows how statistical techniques can be used to draw conclusions from customer responses to survey questionnaires. This paragraph requires the validity of the techniques to be reviewed regularly.

F.10 Help Desk

F.10.1 ISO 9001

4.4.6 *Design changes*

The Help Desk may receive customer requests for change, suggestions for service improvement, complaints and incidents which may lead to requests for change. The procedures need to include a mechanism for identifying and documenting these requests, so that they can be controlled in the same way as other design changes.

4.9.2 *Special processes*

The Help Desk service qualifies as a "special process" because its results cannot be *fully* verified by subsequent inspection and testing. Continuous monitoring is needed in order to make sure that it is meeting the specified requirements.

4.13 *Control of nonconforming product*

Where the service is reported as nonconforming (hardware failure, software fault, slow performance for example) one of the Help Desk's objectives is to restore normal service as quickly as possible and with minimal impact on the user community. The module shows how the Help Desk, Problem Management and Change Management functions combine to accomplish this.

The module explains how, if diagnosis confirms a defect in the service, all affected customers should be informed of what remedial action is required. For example, if the defect is serious then the service may need to be withdrawn until the defect is removed. Otherwise a warning to customers of the existence of the defect, and the recommended avoidance action, may be sufficient.

4.14 *Corrective action*

The Help Desk, in conjunction with Problem Management staff, is particularly responsible for the process defined in sub-paragraph (a): for investigating the cause of non-conforming product/service and the corrective action needed to prevent recurrence.

4.16 *Quality records*

Quality records include incident records, customer satisfaction monitoring data, the records of any testing or calibration of help desk tools, audit reports, training records and quality cost reports.

4.17 *Internal quality audits*

Any Help Desk function should be a subject of internal quality audits to establish whether its activities comply with the established procedures and to determine the effectiveness of the quality system. See section 5 of the module.

4.18 *Training*

Those responsible for Help Desk activities need to be "qualified on the basis of appropriate education, training and/or experience". The module (sections 3 and 5) provides guidance.

4.20 *Statistical techniques*

The module shows how statistics can be used in analysing usage of the Help Desk service. If the results are used to draw conclusions about service quality then the validity of the statistical techniques in use needs to be reviewed regularly.

Annex F
How the ITIL functions and modules relate to ISO 9000

F.11 IT Services Organization

F.11.1 ISO 9001

4.1.2.1	*Responsibility and authority*

The organization structure and the job descriptions of the personnel need to take account of the requirements of this paragraph.

4.1.2.3	*Management representative*

A member of the service organization must be appointed in accordance with this paragraph.

4.2	*Quality system*

The requirements of this paragraph need to be taken into account in setting up the organization. For example:

* documented quality system procedures and instructions are needed

* controls are needed to ensure the quality system is implemented effectively, so that the organization's overall quality objectives are achieved.

Ideally, the quality system should be an integrated process, applied throughout the entire service lifecycle, thus ensuring that quality is "built in" rather than being implemented at the end of the development or delivery process. The emphasis should be on problem prevention, as opposed to correction after occurrence.

4.4.2	*Design and development planning*

The organization needs to identify those responsible for each service design and development activity.

4.6.2	*Assessment of sub-contractors*

This paragraph states the basis on which sub-contractors should be selected and the need to maintain records.

In establishing the organization, the department needs to address how these requirements will be met; for example: what is the likely requirement for sub-contractors? how will sub-contractors be chosen? to what extent will individual managers be permitted to choose their sub-contractors? what information about each subcontractor needs to be recorded?

4.9.1 *Process control - general*

The organization structure is also likely to be affected by this paragraph. It requires the service supplier to identify and plan those service delivery processes which directly affect quality, and to ensure that they are carried out under controlled conditions, examples of which are given.

4.18 *Training*

The service supplier is required to establish and maintain procedures for identifying training needs and ensuring that all relevant personnel have the necessary skills and experience for their respective jobs.

The organization must at the outset, possess the appropriate skill levels. In addition, for skill levels to be maintained, the organization structure and the quality system need to ensure that training requirements are regularly reviewed, by, for example, setting up a training unit and/or conducting formal reviews of job requirements and the skill levels of each job holder.

F.12 Management of Local Processors and Terminals

F.12.1 ISO 9001

4.3 *Contract review*

Section 3 of the module stresses the importance of planning how local processing is to be managed, in the context of delivering an overall service which matches the customer's needs. Agreement needs to be reached between the customer and the service supplier on, for example, the resources to be managed and the division of responsibilities.

This agreement should be subject to the review process described in this paragraph.

4.6.1 *Purchasing - general*
4.6.3 *Purchasing data*

Section 3 of the module suggests how procurement should be managed. The resultant purchasing procedures need to ensure that the requirements of these paragraphs are satisfied.

4.6.2 *Assessment of sub-contractors*

Similarly the selection of sub-contractors (for local PC training or support, for example) should be controlled in accordance with this paragraph.

| | 4.6.4 | *Verification of purchased product* |

The service supplier or customer may wish to verify at source that purchased product (terminal hardware, software upgrade, etc) conforms to specified requirements, as described in this paragraph.

| | 4.9.1 | *Process control - general* |

Procedures are needed which define the tasks local staff need to carry out in order to provide a quality service to users of local terminals. These will have been specified during the service development phase, and will typically include: start/end of day procedures, loading magnetic media, stationery changes, data back-ups, security procedures.

| | 4.10.1 | *Receiving inspection and testing* |

Annex C of the module recommends the use of a standard script for checking newly delivered items. This should be used to develop an inspection and testing procedure which should also comply with the requirements of this paragraph.

| | 4.15 | *Handling, storage, packaging and delivery* |

This paragraph is relevant if the service supplier is responsible for delivering local hardware or software items to the customer or if local arrangements need to be made for storage, prior to use.

F.13 Managing Facilities Management

F.13.1 ISO 9001

| | 4.2 | *Quality system* |

If IT services are supplied to the customer by a Facilities Management (FM) contractor managed by a Service Control Team (SCT) then the SCT should establish a quality system in line with the requirements of this paragraph. The cost of this process is likely to be substantially reduced if the FM supplier has already established a suitable quality system.

| | 4.6.1 | *Purchasing - general* |

The SCT is responsible for ensuring that the FM supplier delivers a service which conforms to the customer's requirements, which need to reflected in the Service Level Agreement.

| | 4.6.2 | *Assessment of sub-contractors* |

The module recommends the use of the standard competitive tender process to select the most appropriate FM supplier. The requirements of this paragraph should also be taken into account when considering potential suppliers.

| | 4.6.3 | *Purchasing data* |

The SCT should ensure that documents (such as SLAs) which specify services to be purchased from the FM supplier comply with this paragraph.

| | 4.6.4 | *Verification of purchased product* |

Provided it is specified in the FM contract the SCT, as a representative of the customer, has "the right to verify at source or upon receipt that purchased product conforms to specified requirements". For example this could be applied to support staff supplied as part of the service or to hardware or software items before they are introduced into the live service.

| | 4.7 | *Purchaser supplied product* |

Where the customer organization (through the SCT) supplies hardware or software for use by the FM service supplier, the FM supplier is responsible for establishing and maintaining procedures for the verification, storage and maintenance of this product. Nevertheless, it is the customer's responsibility to provide acceptable product.

F.14 Network Services Management

F.14.1 ISO 9001

| | 4.15 | *Handling, storage, packaging and delivery* |

This paragraph is relevant if the service supplier is responsible for delivering network hardware or software items to the customer or if local arrangements need to be made for storage, prior to use.

Annex F
How the ITIL functions and modules relate to ISO 9000

F.15 Planning and Control

F.15.1 ISO 9001

4.1.1 *Quality policy*

Defining the organization's quality policy, as described in this paragraph, is a fundamental part of the planning process. Identifying and communicating its objectives will provide focus for the design and development of the quality system.

A clear, agreed quality policy should also influence the attitudes of all personnel within the organization so that they share a common commitment to deliver a quality service to the customer.

4.1.2.2 *Verification resources and personnel*

The planning process should also address how verification is to be carried out, as specified in this paragraph; for example, what is the scale of the verification task? who will do it? what resources do the staff need?

4.2 *Quality system*

The establishment of a quality system, as defined in this paragraph, is also a key part of the planning process. As well as helping the organization and its staff to plan their activities, the quality system will include procedures to control the service development and delivery processes, to ensure that the service delivered to the customer meets the agreed quality standards.

4.4.2 *Design and development planning*

The organization's plans for service design and development need to comply with the requirements of this paragraph; qualified personnel and adequate resources are needed, together with interfaces between groups for effective exchange of information.

Use of the SSADM and PRINCE methods is recommended.

4.4.5 *Design verification*

Similarly, the planning process needs to address the requirements for verification of the service design, as specified in this paragraph.

	4.9.1	*Process control - general*

Planning and Control needs to take account of this paragraph, which requires the organization to identify and plan the service development and delivery processes. It also specifies some of the controls which should be applied.

Use of the SSADM and PRINCE methods is recommended.

	4.14	*Corrective action*

The organization will need effective corrective action procedures if quality IT services are to be provided economically, efficiently and effectively. These procedures should address the requirements of this paragraph.

	4.17	*Internal quality audits*

The planning process must take account of the requirements of this paragraph for carrying out a "comprehensive system of planned and documented internal quality audits".

	4.20	*Statistical techniques*

The planning and control process needs to address the requirements of this paragraph: that, where statistical techniques are to be used, they are adequate to verify the acceptability of process capability and product/service characteristics.

F.16 Problem Management

F.16.1 ISO 9001

	4.4.6	*Design changes*

The problem management process may establish that a configuration item (CI) is defective and needs changing. The problem management procedures must ensure that any changes and modifications are dealt with in accordance with this paragraph.

Problem Management staff may also receive customer requests for change, suggestions for service improvement, complaints and incidents which may lead to requests for change. The procedures need to include a mechanism for identifying and documenting these requests, so that they can be controlled in the same way as other design changes.

	4.10.1	*Receiving inspection and testing*

The module stresses the importance of the relationship between the Problem Management and Change Management functions. Changes introduced to the service to remove defects would normally be the subject of change management procedures. However, involving Problem Management staff in receiving inspection and testing of changed CIs (given their understanding of the problem the change is intended to resolve) is likely to increase the chance of successful resolution.

Problem management procedures should address the requirements of sub-paragraph 2 which states the control necessary when urgent changes are introduced to the service, to correct a critical software fault for example.

4.10.2 *In-process inspection and testing*

As in the case of paragraph 4.10.1 Problem Management staff should work in conjunction with the Change Management function to ensure that changed CIs remove defects as intended.

4.12 *Inspection and test status*

The problem management system must include procedures for recording known errors in CIs, in accordance with this paragraph. If a configuration management (CM) system is in use then the inspection and test status of CIs should be recorded in the CM database.

4.13 *Control of nonconforming product*

The system for recording known errors in CIs needs to comply with the requirements of this paragraph. A CM system should be used where possible.

Note that defective CIs must be prevented from inadvertent use and that control must be provided for the "notification of functions concerned". This means that all affected customers need to be informed of the presence of the defect and of what remedial action is required. If the defect is serious then the service may need to be withdrawn until the defect is removed. Otherwise a warning to customers of the existence of the defect, and the recommended avoidance action, may be sufficient.

The assessment of a problem's severity (and therefore the action needed) is part of the problem management process. Communication with affected customers would normally be the responsibility of the Help Desk function.

	4.14	Corrective action
		Problem Management, in conjunction with the Help Desk function, is particularly responsible for the processes defined in sub-paragraphs (a) and (c): for investigating the cause of non-conforming product/service and initiating the appropriate corrective action(s) needed to prevent recurrence.

F.17 Service Level Management

F.17.1 ISO 9001

	4.1.2.2	Verification resources and personnel
		To develop services which meet Service Level Requirements (SLRs) and monitor their compliance with Service Level Agreements (SLAs), "adequate resources and trained personnel" are needed. Requirements cover service design, development and delivery.
		Any design review (a PRINCE quality review for example) or audit of the SLM function should be carried out by personnel independent of those carrying out the function.
	4.3	Contract review
		Service level management must assist service development projects (supported by other relevant functions such as Availability Management, Capacity Management, Computer Operations Management) to ensure that SLRs are adequately defined and documented, and that IT Services has the capability to meet the requirements.
		Service management should also be prepared to "bridge the knowledge gap" between IT and user by assisting the customer to identify and define his service requirements.
	4.4.3	Design input
		This paragraph requires that design inputs relating to the product/service be identified and documented. Design inputs will include SLRs or constraints.
	4.4.4	Design output
		This paragraph requires that design output shall: (b) contain or reference acceptance criteria and (d) identify those characteristics of the design that are crucial to the safe and proper functioning of the product. SLRs will normally be specified (see preceding paragraph) and form part of the

Annex F
How the ITIL functions and modules relate to ISO 9000

user and/or operational acceptance criteria and, because of their potential effect on service quality, would be amongst those characteristics which are crucial to the proper functioning of the service.

4.4.5 *Design verification*

The SLM function must verify that the service design meets the SLRs (design input requirements) using design control measures such as those described in this paragraph. This subject is addressed in section 3 of the module and is likely also to involve Availability, Capacity and Cost Management staff.

4.6.1 *Purchasing - general*

The service supplier is responsible for ensuring that purchased product and services (hardware maintenance, air conditioning, for example) conform to specified requirements. Where availability or performance requirements have been specified for purchased products (see paragraph 4.6.3), the Availability or Capacity Management function must then ensure that the products/services meet these requirements.

4.6.2 *Assessment of sub-contractors*

The use of contract staff or SLM consultants to assist with the establishment, review, modification or operation of the SLM function must be controlled in accordance with this paragraph. Section 3 and Annex C of the module outline the job requirements for the SLM function.

4.6.3 *Purchasing data*

Availability/reliability requirements should be included in any Operational Requirement or Invitation to Tender issued. Where an SLM function exists it should contribute to the definition of these requirements and the drafting and negotiation of contractual agreements with suppliers.

4.6.4 *Verification of purchased product*

This paragraph emphasises that it is the responsibility of the service supplier, not the customer, to ensure that purchased product (service components) meet individual service requirements (performance, reliability etc).

4.9.2 *Special processes*

The software/service design and construction process comes under this heading. This means that continuous monitoring of live services is required to ensure that they meet their SLRs. The monitoring requirements for a service should be set out in the service quality plan, together with appropriate procedures to ensure that SLRs are met.

4.10.2 *In-process inspection and testing*

Service management should monitor the service delivered to the customer, in accordance with the requirements of this paragraph.

4.10.4 *Inspection and test records*

SLM monitoring data and reports count as inspection and test records which show compliance with the defined SLRs. They are also quality records to which paragraph 4.16 applies.

4.11 *Inspection measuring and test equipment*

"Equipment" in this context also means any software tools used for SLM (see section 7 of the module).

4.14 *Corrective action*

Where SLRs are not being met, the SLM function is responsible for corrective action as defined in this paragraph.

4.16 *Quality records*

Quality records comprise all testing and monitoring data (availability, performance etc), records of any testing or calibration of SLM tools, audit reports, training records and quality cost reports.

4.17 *Internal quality audits*

Any SLM function should be a subject of internal quality audits to establish whether SLM activities comply with the established procedures and to determine the effectiveness of the quality system. This is addressed in section 5 of the module.

4.18 *Training*

SLM activities affect service quality. Personnel performing SLM tasks should be "qualified on the basis of appropriate education, training and/or experience". Sections 3 and 5 of the module give guidance on SLM job requirements.

4.20 *Statistical techniques*

Statistical techniques are used in specifying SLAs and measuring service performance and are therefore subject to the requirements of this paragraph.

F.18 Software Control and Distribution Management

F.18.1 ISO 9001

> 4.9.1 *Process control - general*
>
> This paragraph requires the service supplier to identify and plan the processes which comprise the software control and distribution activity and to ensure that they are properly controlled.
>
> Configuration management should be considered as a method of controlling this process.
>
> 4.10.2 *In-process inspection and testing*
>
> Procedures are needed to ensure that the software control and distribution processes are monitored in accordance with this paragraph, for example, to check for media failures during software replication.
>
> 4.12 *Inspection and test status*
>
> The status of all items (software and documentation) needs to be identified as set out in this paragraph. A configuration management system should be considered for this purpose.
>
> 4.15 *Handling, storage, packaging and delivery*
>
> Procedures are needed to control the handling, storage (locally at the point of issue and on the customer's site if necessary), packaging and delivery of software and documentation (manuals, installation instructions etc).

F.19 Software Lifecycle Support

F.19.1 ISO 9001

> 4.4.3 *Design input*
>
> The design requirements which are input to the software design process need to be controlled in accordance with this paragraph.
>
> The module stresses the importance of including requirements other than functionality: security, quality, performance, capacity and maintainability for example.

	4.7	*Purchaser supplied product*

Section 3 and Annex E of the module explain how to apply lifecycle support techniques to existing systems, for example, in situations where the service supplier is taking over application software previously developed and maintained by the customer.

This paragraph defines the need for verifying such software.

	4.8	*Product identification and traceability*

This paragraph states the requirement for procedures which allow software product (such as program units) to be traceable back to specifications, throughout the lifecycle (development, testing, maintenance etc). The lifecycle model chosen by the service supplier needs to be checked against this requirement.

F.20 Supplier Management

F.20.1 ISO 9001

	4.3	*Contract review*

The procedures for contract review need to ensure that the customer's requirements are adequately defined and that the service supplier is capable of meeting them. In many instances subcontractors will be involved in providing the service to the customer; examples include terminal hardware provision, telecommunications, software development, hardware and software maintenance. Involving them in the contract review stage may assist the service supplier in meeting the requirements of this paragraph.

	4.6.1	*Purchasing - general*
	4.6.3	*Purchasing data*

Procedures are required to ensure that purchasing documents clearly describe the products and services ordered by the supplier and that those products and services conform to specified requirements.

This implies that the requirements need to be adequately specified. For example, the service requirements specified to the hardware maintenance supplier need to reflect the service requirements of the customer.

| | 4.6.2 | *Assessment of sub-contractors* |

Whatever method is used to select sub-contracted suppliers (previously used by the customer, CCTA approved etc) the procedures for sub-contractor selection need to comply with the requirements of this paragraph.

F.21 Testing Software for Operational Use

F.21.1 ISO 9001

| | 4.1.2.2 | *Verification resources and personnel* |

Testing procedures need to address the requirements of this paragraph: that testing requirements (criteria), adequate resources (including terminals, machine capacity etc) and suitably qualified personnel be identified. Note also that testing must be carried out by personnel independent of those directly responsible for the software development.

| | 4.6.1 | *Purchasing - general* |
| | 4.6.3 | *Purchasing data* |

Procedures are required to ensure that purchasing documents clearly describe the software product(s) ordered by the service supplier and that those products conform to specified requirements.

This implies that the requirements need to be adequately specified. This specification may, for example, simply be a product name and version number in the case of PC word processing software, or a requirements specification in the case of bespoke software.

| | 4.6.4 | *Verification of purchased product* |

This paragraph emphasises that it is the responsibility of the service supplier, not the customer, to ensure that purchased software meets the specified requirements. In the case of bespoke software the service supplier should consider verifying the product before it leaves the software developer's premises, subject to his agreement.

| | 4.7 | *Purchaser supplied product* |

Where the customer supplies software for use in the IT service, the service supplier is responsible for establishing and maintaining procedures for its verification and maintenance. This would apply, for example, to existing application software being taken over by the service supplier.

Nevertheless, it remains the customer's responsibility to provide acceptable products.

4.9.1 *Process control - general*

The testing process needs to be planned in accordance with the requirements of this paragraph. For example, work instructions are required which guide staff in how to draw up test plans: what needs testing? what data should be used? what are the acceptance criteria?

4.10.1 *Receiving inspection and testing*

The requirements and acceptance criteria for any purchased software product (package or bespoke) should have been defined prior to purchase (see paragraphs 4.6.1 and 4.6.3). This paragraph requires the service supplier to ensure that the delivered product conforms to the specified requirements.

The paragraph allows for software to be "released for urgent production purposes" provided that it is "positively identified and recorded in order to permit immediate recall .... in the event of nonconformance". A configuration management system should be used for this purpose.

4.10.3 *Final inspection and testing*

The test plan and procedures for testing the final software product before incorporation into the operational service need to comply with the requirements of this paragraph.

4.11 *Inspection, measuring and test equipment*

Any software or hardware tools used to facilitate testing (test harnesses, transaction processing simulators etc) need to be subject to a verification programme as described in this paragraph.

4.13 *Control of nonconforming product*

This paragraph requires that any product which fails to conform to specified requirements is prevented from inadvertent use or introduction into the operational service, and that suitable controls are in place to ensure this. This is best achieved through the use of a configuration management system.

Annex F
How the ITIL functions and modules relate to ISO 9000

F.22 Third Party and Single Source Maintenance Management

F.22.1 ISO 9001

4.3	*Contract review*

The procedures for contract review need to ensure that the customer's requirements are adequately defined and that the service supplier is capable of meeting them. Comparing the contract against the service requirements checklist given in Annex C of the module will help the service supplier comply with the requirements of this paragraph.

Involving Third Party and Single Source Maintenance (SSM) suppliers in contract review will also confirm whether the customer's requirements can be met, particularly if some of the configuration items are obsolete and potentially unmaintainable.

4.6.1	*Purchasing - general*

This paragraph states the service supplier's responsibility for ensuring that the purchased maintenance service conforms to the specified requirements.

4.6.2	*Assessment of sub-contractors*

Section 3 of the module suggests methods of identifying potential maintenance service suppliers. Whatever method is used to select the supplier, the procedure needs to comply with the requirements of this paragraph.

4.6.3	*Purchasing data*

Annex C of the module suggests some mandatory service requirements which should be referenced in purchasing documents (the Operational Requirement for example). Purchasing documents should also be checked for conformance against the requirements of this paragraph.

4.6.4	*Verification of purchased product*

This paragraph reminds the IT Services organization of its right, subject to mutual agreement, to verify the SSM supplier's service "at source". Accordingly the module encourages departments to visit reference sites and the supplier's premises.

Note that such visits do not absolve the SSM supplier of the responsibility to provide acceptable service.

Annex G. ISO 9000 certification

This annex explains the role of accreditation and certification bodies and then describes the process of assessment.

G.1 Accreditation

The European Community in its EN 45000 series of standards has laid down a framework for product and process certification in which organizations issuing certificates are themselves required to be accredited by a National Body according to defined Criteria.

Within the UK the National Body is the National Accreditation Council for Certification Bodies (NACCB).

The role of the NACCB is to review and assess the systems and procedures used by an applicant certification body and to observe and monitor the performance of the certification body's assessors during audits. They may then accredit the certification body in respect of a given industry classification or scope. (A certification body may issue certificates covering various industry sectors, for some of which it may be accredited and for others not.)

G.2 Certification

A certification body is an organization which sets itself up as a supplier of product, service or process certification against established specifications or standards. In the case of Quality Management Systems this is generally related to the ISO 9000/BS 5750 series. There are also some industry sectors which have supplementary criteria agreed by the industry.

A certificate issued by a certification body attests that the assessed organization is operating a QMS compliant with given standards. Only if the NACCB has accredited the certification body for that scope may the NACCB mark be used.

When observing certification body auditors in the field, the NACCB are concerned to determine that the auditors are following good practice, are exercising diligence in their enquiries but are not requiring more, in a quality system, than is necessary, and are applying the standard and guidelines correctly.

G.3 Assessment

Assessment is the review and auditing of an organization's QMS to determine that it meets the requirements of the standards, that it is implemented and that it is effective. It should be a very thorough examination involving all work areas and all activities. Even so the assessment will still be just a sample.

Success or failure

During the course of an assessment, the audit team may uncover a number of non-conformities. These are commonly graded major and minor. A minor non-conformity is a situation where, whilst the procedure, standard or contract is generally being complied with, an exception has been found. A major non-conformity may be the absence of a significant part of the quality system (for example no design reviews are conducted at all) or a large number of instances of failure or non-conformity with an existing feature of the quality system, such that the system is commonly not followed.

With certification bodies, one major non-conformity is sufficient to result in failure. There is not normally any fixed number of minor non-conformities which will cause failure. The decision will be based on the overall picture. Sometimes certification will be conditional upon the auditee company clearing all recorded non-conformities within a short period, say two to three months, when a follow-up audit may be conducted. Whether the result, ie. unconditional success, conditional success or failure, is made known to the auditee company's management at the closing meeting, depends on the practice of the particular certification body.

Where failure occurs, the extent of the failure will determine whether a partial or full re-assessment is required before certification may be granted.

Surveillance

A certification body not only assesses the quality system, it makes periodic visits to check that the system continues to be used and developed. These surveillance visits occur at an agreed rate, typically twice per year, and at relatively short notice - typically one or two weeks.

A surveillance visit is typically for one or two days and one or two auditors may be used at most. The scope of surveillance visits is thus limited and the audit sample confined to a subset of the organization's operations.

Annex G
ISO 9000 certification

Certain areas are considered mandatory for every surveillance visit and these include:

* changes in the system, procedures, or facilities
* changes in the organization or business scope
* internal audits, management review and corrective action (in particular with reference to the previous visit and to customer complaints).

In addition some elements of the quality system standard such as management review and complaints handling are usually reviewed on each visit. The remaining elements are examined over the three year cycle at a frequency appropriate to the organization's scope.

Re-assessment and re-certification

The quality system will be re-assessed as a whole once every three years. Whether this requires as comprehensive as assessment as the original one will depend upon the extent of:

* changes in business and scope
* changes in size and organization
* adoption of new tools and technology
* the experience of surveillance visits.

Large changes in scope or size, such as occasioned by a take-over or major re-organization, may precipitate a re-assessment in less than three years.

Annex H. Types of quality audit

This annex describes types of quality audit.

There are three major types of quality audit, which are used in different circumstances:

* first party or internal audits
* second party or external supplier audits
* third party audits.

H.1 First party audits

First party audits or internal audits are audits carried out by an organization itself continuously to assess its quality system; these are a key requirement of ISO 9000 standards.

First party audits must be carried out by members of staff trained in quality auditing techniques and must be independent of the activities being reviewed.

First party audits can be carried out for a number of reasons in addition to the ISO 9000 requirements as follows:

* to provide evidence of quality improvements and QMS effectiveness
* to enable management to identify areas for improvement
* to find out and correct deficiencies before a customer or assessment body finds them
* in response to departmental project requests
* to improve communication and QMS understanding
* as a training exercise for staff and new auditors
* to enable staff to discuss problems they have for which the solution is outside their control.

A National Registration Scheme for Internal Auditors of Quality Systems has recently been set up by the Institute of Quality Assurance. Full details of the requirements for registration are set out in a booklet, ref RBA/169/92/1 available from the IQA in Southwark Street, London SE1 1SB.

H.2 Second party audits

Second party audits or external supplier audits are those where an IT Services organization is either assessed by an external customer or purchasing organization and is normally restricted to the scope of the supplied service, or where the IT Services organization itself conducts audits in the departments which provide it with products or service. (The concept of the cross-department or cross-function audit can be very useful for assessing areas for quality improvement!) It is usual for a certificate of compliance or conformance to be issued by the auditing company or department as a result of successful external supplier audits.

H.3 Third party audits

Third party audits can be of two types:

* audits of an supplier organization's QMS carried out by an external company on behalf of either the organization's management if no internal auditing function has been set up, or on behalf of a customer, to provide an independent assessment of the supplier's suitability for contracts. This type of audit is a third party external audit.

* audits carried out by third party companies with the express intention of assessing the IT Services organization against a given QMS standard. In such cases the third party organization has a contract purely to carry out and report on the audit. Such audits are called "Extrinsic Audits" and are carried out by certification bodies and often lead to ratification to an ISO 9000 standard for a defined scope of service provision.

For further discussion of these audit types, reference should be made to the QMS Audit volume of the QML.

Annex I. Interdependence of ITIL functions/modules

This annex describes the relationships between each of the appropriate IT Infrastructure Library functions and modules and considers the importance of each of the functions, and the guidance in the other modules, to a Quality Management System (QMS) for IT Services.

The appropriate ITIL service management functions are: availability management, capacity management, computer operations management, configuration management, contingency planning, cost management, customer liaison, help desk, network services management, operational test management, planning and control, problem management, service level management and software control and distribution. Other ITIL modules which provide additional related guidance in support of these functions are: **Computer Installation and Acceptance**, **IT Services Organization**, **Management of Local Processors and Terminals**, **Managing Facilities Management**, **Managing Supplier Relationships**, **Software Lifecycle Support**, **Testing Software for Operational Use** and **Third Party and Single Source Maintenance**.

The annex provides the basis for the suggested implementation sequence set out in Section 3.4.

For each function/module it answers the questions:

* how does this function/module relate to other IT Infrastructure Library functions and modules?

* how important is this function or guidance to my proposed QMS?

Each function/module is discussed in alphabetic order below. For a more detailed evaluation of each function against the international standard (ISO 9000) see Annex F.

I.1 Availability management

Availability management is the optimization of the availability of IT infrastructures and the supporting organization providing IT services to ensure that the requirements of the customers of the service are met.

Availability management supports service level management during service specification, design, development and delivery by supplying availability data and forecasts. As noted in Annex F (Availability Management ISO 9001 4.4.4), availability requirements will be among those characteristics which will be crucial to the proper functioning of the service. (**Software Lifecycle Support** discusses the need to consider availability and security requirements at every stage of service specification, development and use.)

Availability management also supports the procurement of hardware, software and services by assisting with the specification of availability/reliability/ serviceability requirements, and will be responsible for monitoring supplier (sub-contractor) compliance with contractual conditions on serviceability. (See **Third Party and Single Source Maintenance** and **Managing Supplier Relationships**.)

In carrying out these specification, development and procurement roles, the Availability Management function will need to liaise with the IT Planning Unit, Capacity Management, Cost Management, Computer Operations Management and Network Services Management, on the plans for new IT services to ensure that services are planned and managed to meet availability/reliability, capacity/performance and cost requirements. The IT Planning Unit will also require availability data and forecasts for strategic and tactical planning, as will the Contingency Planning function.

Availability management is supported by:

* configuration management - the identification and recording of system components is a key element in monitoring, and reporting on, availability

* data from problem management and the help desk

* change management - ill considered and uncontrolled change is a major source of reduced availability

* computer operations and network services management where well designed policies, procedures and configurations can be a major contributory factor to high availability

* customer liaison - effective communication with customers is important in servicing availability requirements.

The achievement of availability requirements should be tested during operational testing (**Testing an IT Service for Operational Use**).

Annex I
Interdependence of ITIL functions/modules

Other relevant guidance is given in the IT Infrastructure Library modules on **Accommodation Specification**, **Secure Power Supplies** and **Specification and Management of a Cable Infrastructure**.

The Availability Management function contributes to IT service quality assurance by:

* advising the IT Directorate, Service Level Management and application development teams on issues regarding availability which helps to ensure that specified IT service requirements are realistic

* ensuring that the availability requirements of new services can be met, and that those of existing services continue to be met which will involve both contract (SLA) review and ongoing service performance analysis

* monitoring availability, reliability, maintainability and serviceability which contributes to the ISO 9001 requirement [4.10.2(b)] to establish product conformance to specified requirements by the use of process monitoring and control methods

* improving availability beyond the required level within cost constraints which contributes to the service improvement obligation imposed by ISO 9004-2 [6.4.4].

Clearly, agreeing, reviewing and monitoring availability does not require that a formal function as described in the IT Infrastructure Library is essential. However all the aspect of availability management described there are highly desirable in terms of assuring service quality.

For the Availability Management function to be fully effective the Help Desk and Problem Management functions should also be implemented since the Availability Management function will wish to analyse incident and problem data in order to try to improve service reliability and availability.

I.2 Capacity management

Capacity management supports the optimum and cost-effective provision of IT services by helping organizations to match their IT resources to the demands of the business.

Capacity management supports service level management during service specification, design, development and delivery by supplying capacity and performance data and forecasts. As noted in Annex D (Capacity Management ISO

9001 4.4.4), capacity requirements will be among those characteristics which will be crucial to the proper functioning of the service. (**Software Lifecycle Support** discusses the need to consider capacity and performance requirements at every stage of service specification, development and use.)

Capacity management also supports the procurement of hardware, software and services by assisting with the specification of capacity and performance requirements, and will be responsible for monitoring supplier (sub-contractor) compliance with contractual conditions on performance. (See **Third Party and Single Source Maintenance** and **Managing Supplier Relationships**.)

In carrying out these specification, development and procurement roles, the Capacity Management function will need to liaise with the IT Planning Unit, Availability Management, Cost Management, Computer Operations Management and Network Services Management, on the plans for new IT services to ensure that services are planned and managed to meet capacity/ performance, availability/reliability and cost requirements. The IT Planning Unit will also require capacity and performance data and forecasts for strategic and tactical planning, as will the Contingency Planning function.

Capacity management is supported by:

* configuration management - the identification and recording of system components is a key element in monitoring, and reporting on, capacity and performance

* data from problem management and the help desk

* change management - ill considered and uncontrolled change is a major source of reduced performance

* computer operations and network services management where well designed policies, procedures and configurations can be a major contributory factor to high performance

* customer liaison - effective communication with customers is important in servicing capacity and performance requirements.

The achievement of capacity and performance requirements should be tested during operational testing .

Annex I
Interdependence of ITIL functions/modules

I.3 Change management

Change management is an essential component of configuration management (see below).

I.4 Computer installation and acceptance

The **Computer Installation and Acceptance** module of the IT Infrastructure Library gives guidance on the planning and installation of new equipment and software.

I.5 Computer operations management

Computer operations management is the organization and conduct of computer operations to provide quality IT services which satisfy the organizations's business needs.

Computer operations management is complemented by service level management. The nature of the IT service to be provided by operations, and the resources needed to do it are determined by the contents of SLAs and service quality plans. The satisfactory achievement of agreed service levels depends, in part, on the quality of computer operations (Ops). Ideally, Ops will support the Service Level Manager during service specification, design and development.

Ops works closely with the Help Desk and Problem Management team to handle IT service incidents. Ideally using a common system based on a configuration management database to record and progress incidents and problems.

Ops is complemented by Network Services Management. Procedures for the operation of computer and telecommunications systems should be complementary.

The controlled implementation of change is essential to minimize risk to IT services. The **Change Management** module gives guidance on how changes to IT services should be managed.

Ops should be involved in the preparation and testing of contingency plans. The **Contingency Planning** module gives guidance on the plans required.

Ops is often responsible for ensuring that only authorised software releases are used to provide a live service. The **Software Control and Distribution** module covers the replication (production), release (delivery) and implementation (installation) of software.

Operability standards need to be formulated and agreed with users. The behaviour of Ops can affect users (in particular their perception of the quality of the service) and vice versa. Regular reviews should take place and any necessary corrective action should be instigated. The Customer Liaison module covers these issues.

Ops may be given devolved responsibility for monitoring system performance, reporting on exceptions and problems to the Capacity Management team, and for day to day performance tuning activities under the overall control of the Capacity Manager. The Capacity Management module includes guidance on performance monitoring and system tuning.

A number of activities which are often the responsibility of Ops are described in the **Computer Installation and Acceptance** module.

Ops is normally responsible for ensuring that the contracted maintenance of equipment to help to sustain the availability of IT services is carried out, and for managing the recovery after failures.

Ops often has day to day working relationships with suppliers of IT equipment, software, services and consumables. Advice on how these relationships should be conducted is contained in the **Managing Supplier Relationships** module.

Guidance for organizations running, or intending to run, a mixture of attended/unattended of totally unattended systems is given in the **Unattended Operating** module.

Computer operations management is an essential component of a QMS. Ops carries out the process control requirements of ISO 9001 (4.9), and is involved in in-process and final inspection and testing (4.10, 4.11 and 4.12), and in responding to and recovering from incidents and problems (4.13 and 4.14). Ops staff will often be involved in handling and storing purchased product (4.15) and will be required to maintain quality records (4.16).

Clearly defined Ops procedures covering change management, disaster recovery, operability and paragraphs 4.9 to 4.16 of ISO 9001 (see Annex E) are essential to an IT service management QMS. These procedures should be a subject of the configuration management system and thus subject to document control procedures.

I.6 Configuration management

Configuration management is a discipline, normally supported by software tools, that gives IT management control over IT assets (see Annex A).

Configuration management (including change control) supports problem management and Help Desk, availability management, capacity management and cost management, and software control and distribution. It should also be used to control the movement of components into and out of independent testing environments (see **Testing an IT Service for Operational Use**).

Configuration management is an essential component of an IT service QMS.

I.7 Contingency planning

Contingency planning is the planning to cope with, and recover from, an IT disaster, and to safeguard systems to prevent incidents from becoming disasters.

Contingency planning gives guidance on the inclusion of modified service levels in SLAs, which apply when a contingency service is in operation.

The Network Services Management function gives advice on planning networks in order to reduce the risk of disaster. Availability management supports contingency planning by providing information on managing the risk of component failure, and on maintaining high availability. These practices can be used to provide "resilience to disaster". The Capacity Management function will provide guidance on the sizing of a replacement system to provide critical services.

The Customer Liaison function can help to obtain the information from customers required to prepare a contingency plan.

Configuration management supports contingency planning, by assisting with the production and maintenance of an IT asset register.

Contingency planning helps to ensure that an agreed level of service provision is maintained in the event of a disaster or serious incident and so helps to maintain service quality.

I.8 Cost management

Cost management addresses the management accounting required for IT Services, and the pricing of and charging for IT services.

The Cost Management function supplies the information needed by senior management for effective planning and control.

Pricing and charging policies will influence customer perception and use of the service provided, and service charges should be written into SLAs (see **Service Level Management**).

Capacity management (see E2) is concerned with the provision and management of IT capacity to ensure that required service levels can be achieved. The Capacity Managers must be aware of the costs of providing that capacity so that services can be provided cost effectively.

Cost management is supported by configuration management. The configuration management database can be used to record data on the costs of configuration items.

Cost management is a highly desirable part of a QMS for IT Services.

I.9 Customer liaison

Customer liaison is important for IT Services, it helps to ensure that the quality services are being provided, that customer's make the best use of their services, and that IT Services is responsive to customer needs and problems.

The module explains the need for effective communication and cooperation between IT service providers and their customers. It addresses customer support activities (advice and assistance to customers to help them to make the best use of IT services, making IT service providers aware of customers' views and joint determination of future requirements), how to conduct professional customer contacts, and customer liaison initiatives to improve customer satisfaction.

All IT Services staff who are involved with customers have a customer liaison responsibility. Help Desk staff in particular can make an important contribution to customer liaison, and customer liaison staff must work closely together.

Annex I
Interdependence of ITIL functions/modules

The Customer Liaison function can assist with the introduction of change and the change management process, and supports service level management by helping to establish formal relationships with customers.

The processes of customer liaison, problem management, help desk, service level management and change management may be part of a Customer Services function within IT Services.

ISO 9004-2 describes customer assessment of service quality as the ultimate measure of the quality of the service, and requires that service organizations should institute an ongoing assessment and measurement of customer satisfaction. Customer Liaison discusses the purpose, design and analysis of customer survey questionnaires which should form a part of the ongoing assessment and measurement process.

ISO 9004-2 also requires a programme for continuously improving service quality. The module **Customer Liaison** describes initiatives which can assist with this process.

I.10 Help desk

A help desk is a vital part of the interface between IT Services and its customers. A help desk provides first line incident support, day-to-day contact between IT Services and its customers, advice on the use of IT services, management reports on service quality.

A help desk: supports service level management, problem management, availability management and customer liaison. In particular, it is a highly desirable component of a problem management system (the investigation and correction of non-conformities is required by ISO 9001).

I.11 IT Services organization

ISO 9001 requires that the "responsibility, authority and interrelation of all personnel who manage, perform and verify work affecting quality shall be defined". **IT Services Organization** provides guidance on this subject. All other IT Infrastructure Library modules are related to this subject since they describe the activities which should take place, and the staffing required to carry them out.

I.12 Management of local processors and terminals

The **Management of Local Processors and Terminals** module gives guidance on establishing the best division of responsibilities between central (ie IT Services) management and local (ie business) management for the provision of IT facilities within the business areas. This guidance should be considered when defining management responsibility (ISO 9001 4.1).

It is supported by the **Customer Liaison**, **Help Desk**, **Change Management**, **Configuration Management**, **Problem Management**, **Network Services Management**, **Service Level Management**, **Software Control and Distribution**, **Managing Supplier Relationships**, **Third Party and Single Source Maintenance**, **Cost Management for IT Services**, **Testing an IT Service for Operational Use**, **Contingency Planning** and **Capacity Management** modules.

I.13 Managing facilities management

The **Managing Facilities Management** module gives advice to organizations considering the use of a facilities management (FM) arrangement to provide IT services. As such, all the other IT Infrastructure Library functions and modules are relevant. However, the **Service Level Management** module is particularly important as it provides guidance on how to frame service level requirements for an FM provider, and on the SLAs which will form the basis of the contract.

I.14 Managing supplier relationships

The **Managing Supplier Relationships** module gives guidance on managing the IT service organization's relationships with IT infrastructure component suppliers and maintainers. Supplier (sub-contractor) actions and activities may be critical to IT service quality.

I.15 Network services management

The **Network Services Management** module gives guidance on the planning, implementation, and on-going management of networks and network services.

The **Service Level Management** module gives guidance on the operation and use of SLAs. The Network Manager will be a party to these agreements, and must deliver the agreed quality of service.

It is possible that the network could be managed on a facilities management basis. See **Managing Facilities Management**.

Network services management will be supported by capacity management, cost management, availability management, contingency planning, configuration management, change management, problem management and help desk.

The Network Services Manager and the Computer Operations Manager must work closely together to provide the services required and to resolve incidents and problems.

The **Managing Supplier Relationships** and **Third Party and Single Source Maintenance** modules are also relevant.

I.16 Operational testing management

Operational testing management is described in **Testing an IT Service for Operational Use**. This is the equivalent of ISO 9001 4.6.4: verification of purchased product and 4.10.1: Receiving inspection and testing. Operational testing is an essential component of an IT Services QMS.

I.17 Planning and control

Effective planning and control is essential for the successful management of IT Services. The Planning and Control function will draw on information from all IT Infrastructure Library functions.

I.18 Problem management

Problem management supports service level management and service delivery (see **Computer Operations Management**, **Network Services Management** and **Availability Management**).

Problem management is supported by Help Desk and configuration management.

Problem management is an essential component of an IT service QMS (in particular it addresses paragraph 4.14 of ISO 9001: Corrective action).

I.19 Service level management

Service level management is the process of defining, negotiating, contracting, monitoring and reviewing the levels of user service that are both required and cost justified.

Service level management is supported by availability management and third party and single source maintenance which address the contracts and conditions required to ensure reliability and availability. Availability management also addresses the activities needed to ensure that agreed service levels are met.

Capacity management supports service level management by helping to ensure that adequate capacity is always available.

Service level management is also supported by configuration management, change management, Help Desk and problem management.

Customer liaison and managing supplier relationships are also important to managing service levels.

For service level management to be fully effective it is recommended that some form of charging, or notional charging, is made for the services provided (see **Cost Management for IT Services**).

Service level management is an essential part of quality management.

I.20 Software control and distribution

Software control and distribution is part of configuration management. In particular, it addresses the process of software release build, distribution and implementation. Software control and distribution helps to address the requirements of ISO 9000-3 5.9 Replication, 5.10.7 Release procedures and 6.1 Configuration management.

I.21 Software lifecycle support

Software lifecycle support addresses the need for close cooperation between customers of IT Services, IT infrastructure managers and software developers in order to ensure the provision of high quality services. It is an integral part of quality management.

Annex I
Interdependence of ITIL functions/modules

I.22 Testing an IT service for operational use

See operational testing management (I.16).

I.23 Third party and single source maintenance

Third party maintenance (TPM) is the provision of maintenance services for IT equipment and sometimes other facilities by a contractor other than the supplier of the equipment. Single source maintenance (SSM) is the provision of all IT maintenance services in a location of an organization by a single supplier.

The guidance given on TPM and SSM is relevant to the control of purchasing (ISO 9001 4.6) and in particular to the assessment of sub-contractors (4.6.2).

Annex J. IT service quality characteristics

To allow service quality to be evaluated, requirements should be specified in terms of quality characteristics and sub-characteristics. As the service is decomposed into its component parts (hardware, systems software, applications software, procedures, staffing, etc) then the interrelationships between the requirements and each of the components should be determined. (Methods such as QFD (Quality Function Deployment) may help with this process.)

Metrics must be defined that allow the characteristics to be measured (the metrics required may differ during the various stages of the IT service development process), and rating levels - measuring the level of satisfaction of requirements - defined. To assess the quality of the service, the results of the evaluation of the different characteristics must be summarised, and a method for this should be prepared.

Service quality characteristics

IT service quality characteristics are the set of attributes of a service by which its quality is described and evaluated: for example, functionality, reliability, usability, efficiency, efficiency, maintainability, and portability. A service quality characteristic may be refined into multiple levels of sub-characteristics. For example:

* **functionality** may be considered in terms of: *suitability* - the presence and appropriateness of a set of functions for specified tasks; *accuracy* - the provision of correct or agreed results or effects; *interoperability* - the ability to interact with specified systems; *compliance* - adherence to application standards, legislation or similar requirements; and *security* - the ability to prevent either accidental or deliberate unauthorised access to programmes or data

* **efficiency** may be considered in terms of: the *time behaviour* of the system - things such as response times, processing times and throughput rates; and *resource behaviour* the amount of resources used and the length of time they are used for.

ISO/IEC 9126 (1991) gives guidance on software product evaluation - quality characteristics and guidelines for their use. The **Availability Management** module gives guidance on assessing reliability.

IT Infrastructure Library
Quality Management for IT Services

Comments Sheet

CCTA hopes that you find this book both useful and interesting. We will welcome your comments and suggestions for improving it
Please use this form or a photocopy, and continue on a further sheet if needed.

From:

        Name

        Organization

        Address

        Telephone

COVERAGE
Does the material cover your needs?
If not, then what additional material would you like included.

CLARITY
Are there any points which are unclear?
If yes, please detail where and why.

ACCURACY
Please give details of any inaccuracies found.

If more space is required for these or other comments. please continue overleaf

IT Infrastructure Library
Quality Management for IT Services

Comments Sheet

OTHER COMMENTS

**Information Systems Engineering Group
CCTA,
Rosebery Court,
St Andrews Business Park,
Norwich, NR7 0HS**

Further Information

Further information on the contents of this module can be obtained from:

Information Systems Engineering Group
CCTA
Rosebery Court
St Andrews Business Park
Norwich
NR7 0HS

Telephone: 01603 704704
(GTN: 3040 4704)